Your Towns and Cities in

South Devon
in the Great War

Dedicated to Dan Clack, a family friend.
Lieutenant Daniel John Clack,
1st Battalion, The Rifles,
killed in action in Afghanistan on 12 August 2011

Your Towns and Cities in the Great War

South Devon
in the Great War

Tony Rea

Pen & Sword
MILITARY

First published in Great Britain in 2016 by
PEN & SWORD MILITARY
an imprint of
Pen and Sword Books Ltd
47 Church Street
Barnsley
South Yorkshire S70 2AS

ISBN 978 1 47383 425 5

A CIP record for this book is available from the British Library

Printed and bound in England
by CPI Group (UK) Ltd, Croydon, CR0 4YY

Typeset in Times New Roman by Chic Graphics

Pen & Sword Books Ltd incorporates the imprints of
Pen & Sword Archaeology, Atlas, Aviation, Battleground, Discovery,
Family History, History, Maritime, Military, Naval, Politics, Railways,
Select, Social History, Transport, True Crime, Claymore Press,
Frontline Books, Leo Cooper, Praetorian Press, Remember When,
Seaforth Publishing and Wharncliffe.

For a complete list of Pen and Sword titles please contact
Pen and Sword Books Limited
47 Church Street, Barnsley, South Yorkshire, S70 2AS, England
E-mail: enquiries@pen-and-sword.co.uk
Website: www.pen-and-sword.co.uk

Contents

Acknowledgements

Cover photograph (Totnes Image Bank)

Thanks to Richard Beeson; Cookworthy Museum, Kingsbridge; Jill Drysdale; the East Prawle History Society; the Keep Military Museum, Dorchester; the King's Own Royal Regiment Museum, Lancaster; Tom Maddock; Roger Mitchell; John Stacey; Stowford Mill Archives Group, Ivybridge; Totnes Image Bank; Barrie Wilson; Stella Gillingham, all of whom freely provided help.

Introduction

How many citizens of South Devon considered themselves victors by November 1918? Perhaps we shall never know. Relief, grief for fathers, sons, brothers or lovers lost in war, quiet contemplation – these are as likely to have been the overriding emotions away from newspaper headlines. This book attempts to give voice to the unsung heroes and heroines of this area. Within its pages are stories of the hopes, fears, sacrifice and endurance of the men and women of South Devon.

There were occasional, unusual highlights: the accidental shooting of two off-duty officers, a hospital ship torpedoed off the South Devon coast, a British airship crash landing on Dartmoor near Ivybridge. Otherwise life went on, bounded by the seasons, the weather and news from foreign fields.

Geographically the book covers an area that is roughly from the present day eastern boundary of the city of Plymouth to the River Exe, excluding the city of Exeter. This area is roughly bound to the north by Dartmoor and to the south by the sea. It comprises the modern day administrative districts of Teignbridge, Torbay and the South Hams. However, geographic boundaries have not served to impede the telling of a good story and so, at times, the reader is taken beyond these somewhat artificial parameters – and occasionally to distant continents – in order to complete the narrative.

The war broke out in the summer of 1914 and this is as good a starting point as any, though occasionally the narrative turns to events prior to this date in order to make specific points of explanation. Fighting ceased in November 1918 and a peace treaty was signed in the summer of 1919, but wounded servicemen were continuing to die into the 1920s. For convenience the main body of the book finishes in 1918.

Celebrations in Aveton Gifford to mark return of peace. (Cookworthy Museum, Kingsbridge)

That war is now commonly referred to as the First World War, though at the time was known simply as The War or the Great War. Throughout the book the term Great War is used.

South Devon was, in 1914, much as it is now. The main differences being fewer people, smaller towns and villages and the absence of motor vehicles, balanced by a busier railway network.

Devon's population had not grown as rapidly in the nineteenth century as in most other parts of the country. For example, whilst in 1801 Devon was the fourth largest county by population, a hundred years later it had been overtaken and was fifteenth largest. There were exceptions. The coastal 'resort' towns were growing quickly and

A troop train leaving Paignton, 1914. (Totnes Image Bank)

Newton Abbot had expanded as it was a sub-regional railway centre.

Littlehempston, home to Private Barter (see p. 38) remains. Its wartime story is typical of South Devon, a land of small towns and villages, coast and farmland; young men went to fight, horses were requisitioned. Those left behind carried on with the farming and waited. Some houses were eventually used as hospitals or convalescent homes for servicemen, and German PoWs arrived to work on the farms.

There were four or five towns in what is now the district of South Hams (four or five – as it is uncertain as to what constitutes the difference between a large village and a small town). These were Dartmouth, Kingsbridge, Modbury, Salcombe and Totnes; Ivybridge was a small but important industrial village then. In Teignbridge were Ashburton, Bovey Tracey, Buckfastleigh, Newton Abbot and Teignmouth. Then there were the seaside resorts of Dawlish, Torquay and Paignton and the fishing port at Brixham. Every other site of habitation ranged from a large village to a hamlet.

Each of these places was affected, to a lesser or greater degree, by the war. Many young men, some of them Reservists or Territorials, others answering Kitchener's call to arms, went away to fight. Some never came home.

To understand how local life functioned in the early twentieth century and, crucially, how the mobilisation of August 1914 worked – how so many men and their horses were very quickly moved out of south Devon – the reader will need to know more about the contemporary railway network.

As it does now, the Great Western Railway ran west from Exeter to Plymouth – but with five branches and many, many more stations. At Newton Abbot branches thrust north to Heathfield, Bovey Tracey and Mortonhampstead, and south to Torbay and Kingswear. At Totnes a branch line went to Buckfastleigh and Ashburton. At South Brent a substantial branch, known as the Primrose line, went south to Kingsbridge. Shortly before reaching Plymouth, a branch went south-east to Turnchapel and Yealmpton.

In addition, in 1914 it was possible to stand on a platform at Exeter St David's station and witness trains bound for Plymouth setting off in both northerly as well as southerly directions, for the London South Western Railway went to Plymouth via Crediton, Okehampton, Tavistock and Bere Alston. There was also a line from Exeter St David's to Heathfield, which joined the Newton Abbot – Mortonhampstead branch.

Tony Rea
www.tonyrea.co.uk

Bovey Tracey railway station, now the local heritage centre. (Author's collection)

PART 1

Business as Usual?

Can there have been anything approaching life as normal? The war impacted on daily life from the outbreak of hostilities. In August 1914 fishing in Start Bay and the rest of the Channel was halted. A decision was made to abandon the South Devon rugby season due to the large numbers joining up. Belgian refugees had begun to arrive in 1914. One family of Belgians was taken in by the Orlebars of Rutt House, near Ivybridge. In November more Belgians arrived at Sheepleigh Court, Bantham and then, in December, Frogmore. It seemed as though everybody and everything was affected by the war.

In 1914 there were thirty German men of military age living in Buckfast, South Devon. Unlike others of German nationality however, these men were never interned as enemy aliens. They were monks and they lived at Buckfast Abbey, where two-thirds of the monastic community were German.

The medieval abbey at Buckfast fell out of use and into dilapidation after the Reformation. It was re-established in 1882 by Lord Clifford of Chudleigh. By 1884 accurate drawings of the foundations had been made and a plan put forward for the rebuilding of the abbey in the style of the mid-twelfth century, based on studies of other Cistercian abbeys such as Fountains in Yorkshire. The Abbot's Tower had been restored and a temporary church erected next to it. This was opened in March 1884. Work also started on the south wing of the monastery, which was to include the kitchen, refectory and cloister, mostly paid for by Lord Clifford. The Benedictine monks were tasked with serving the local Catholic community as priests, as well as with rebuilding the church.

In 1906 two Buckfast monks, Abbot Boniface Natter and Brother Anscar Vonier, were shipwrecked. Natter drowned, but Vonier survived and was elected as the new Abbot upon his return to the abbey. Abbot Vonier was caught out by the outbreak of war, as he was visiting Austria. The newspapers reported on 25 September that he was *'safe in Salzberg'*.

The building work carried on throughout the Great War, during which time the monks continued to farm their 50 acres of land. The German monks – most of whom had lived at the abbey for more than five years prior to the war, some for as many as twenty years – were prohibited from leaving the monastery without special licence. Of course their nationality made them subjects of suspicion and surveillance, and they had to endure hostility from some of the local population. For example, Buckfastleigh Urban District Council campaigned to have the German monks removed, but the Home Secretary refused to officially intern them.

During the war the monks of Buckfast developed medicines, made cider and supplied the people of Buckfast and nearby Buckfastleigh with firewood. The Abbey's 100 beehives produced upwards of five tonnes of heather honey. In 1919, Abbot Vonier – who had become a naturalised British subject – thanked the Home Office for its consideration in dealing with the monks of the abbey during the war.

The quiet life of monks was touched by the war elsewhere, too. In August 1914 the opening of the new church at Wood Barton Monastery was postponed. Wood Barton, near Woodley, was constructed in 1904 by a Trappist community that moved from France because of anti-Catholic legislation by the Third Republic. Its mother house was at Melleraie. The church opening was postponed because the Abbot of Melleraie, aged 84, was thought to be too old and frail to make a Channel crossing in wartime. More bad news was to follow. On 21 August 1914 the *South Devon and Kingsbridge Gazette* reported that eight of the monks from Wood Barton had been conscripted into the French Army and a further ten were returning to the mother house in France. In June 1915 the same newspaper reported the death of one of those monks, a Father Gabriel. Few monks returned to Wood Barton after the war and the community closed in 1921.

Those who had believed the war would be over quickly were now having to reconsider. The war might be experienced at first hand – rifle ranges were opened up, such as those at Hillside, Kingsbridge and Modbury – or second-hand, through news media. In December 1914 the good people of Kingsbridge saw the bombing of Scarborough by the Germans on film at Kingsbridge 'electric cinema'.

In some ways, however, life did carry on as normal. On 1 October 1915 the *South Devon and Kingsbridge Gazette* carried three war related stories: a local Coldstream Guardsman home on leave, a bravery award for a local soldier and a family with six sons in the army; but it also carried a feature on a local farmer who had grown a potato weighing in at over two pounds!

Recruiting

Many men volunteered for service soon after the war was declared. For example, by April 1915 of the sixty-six men living in Aveton Gifford eligible for military service, sixty had enlisted.

Yet the image of every fit man in the country joining up in August 1914 in order to get a taste of adventure in a war that would be done and dusted by Christmas, is largely mythical. It soon became apparent to the government that not enough fit young men were coming forward to enlist. Joint Parliamentary Recruitment Committees were formed and given the responsibility of ensuring Lord Kitchener got enough recruits to fill his New Army battalions. By November 1914 the number of Devonshire men who had enlisted was approximately half of the national average (4.7% compared to 10.2%).

A crowd in the street at Aveton Gifford on recruiting day, 1914. (Cookworthy Museum, Kingsbridge)

Opposition to recruitment was vicarious. It came from the trade unions and the Independent Labour Party, though these socialist movements may not have had much impact across rural Devon. On the other hand, the voices of those non-conformist clergy who also opposed the war may have rung loud in the ears of many.

The Lord Lieutenant of Devon, Earl Fortescue of Castle Hill, put the blame for resisting the call to arms onto Devonshire farmers, but the picture is more complex. There may have been some truth in Fortescue's criticism, for rural recruitment was lower than that from urban areas at a national level. Also, the declaration of war during the summer harvest meant there was certainly no rush to war by those engaged in agriculture. There were other 'special cases'. For example, soon after the outbreak of war the woollen mills of Buckfastleigh were working flat out producing khaki cloth and not a worker could be spared.

The week ending 5 September 1914 was the nation's biggest recruitment week to date with clergy of the Church of England, politicians and soldiers combining to passionately support recruitment drives and urge men to join up. Devon's recruitment figures were still lower than the national average. In March 1915 Lord Lieutenant Fortescue began to publish the recruitment figures in local newspapers, perhaps in an effort to shame men into enlistment: Widecombe-in-the-Moor was lowest with just 3% of the eligible population having joined up; Chudleigh the highest with 12%.

As the *South Devon and Kingsbridge Gazette* pointed out as early as 21 August 1914, '*British pluck was the same now as it was 100 years ago*', and there was no suggestion that Devon 'pluck' should be any less than average. It should also be remembered that Devon is not just a rural county, but also a maritime area. Compared to inland areas of Britain, a greater proportion of South Devon men joined the navy rather than the army. For example, in Ivybridge – then a small village a railway journey from the coast – of the forty-five men killed in the war, eleven were sailors. It is not unreasonable to assume, then, that roughly twenty-five per cent of men from an area such as this would opt for naval service.

In April 1915 a route march through South Devon over four days by men of the 3rd (Special Reserve) Battalion, the Devonshire Regiment, brought in fifty-six new recruits. The forty men, including a band, who marched were led by Lieutenant G.S.M. Larder who had been wounded in action. They were billeted in South Brent on the night of the 21st and the next day marched to Kingsbridge by a circuitous route, stopping along the way for speeches and refreshments. They left Bittaford at 9.20am bound for Ivybridge, Modbury and Salcombe, reaching the latter at 4.30pm. At 7pm the troops reached Kingsbridge where they were joined by soldiers of the 10th King's Own Royal Lancaster Regiment, who were stationed in the town. Supper was given at the King's Arms.

Reluctance to volunteer can be seen as part of a national trend, however. In 1915 the National Registration Act was created and a

According to the Dartmoor National Park archives this picture shows men of the 3rd (Special Reserve) Battalion departing from Bovey Tracey Town Hall during their recruiting march in 1915. The Totnes Image Bank believes it to be Devonshire Regiment Territorials (possibly the 5th Devons) drilling. The soldiers include W. Harris and Jonas Steer (Totnes Image Bank)

list of all the men fit for military service who were still available was compiled. Conscription was introduced in January 1916, targeting single men aged 18-41. Within a few months this was extended to include married men. Men who were called up for service could appeal to a local Military Service Tribunal. Reasons for appeal against military service included poor health, already doing important war work or moral or religious reasons. The latter group became known as the Conscientious Objectors and these count for 2% of those who appealed. Some Conscientious Objectors were billeted in Dartmoor gaol, Princetown where they worked the local quarries.

Now the horses and men have gone: Agriculture
The British Army of 1914 – 1918 was horse drawn. Horses were needed overwhelmingly for use as draught animals as well as by the

Horses for sale on Kingsbridge Quay in 1914. (Cookworthy Museum, Kingsbridge)

A similar perspective of Kingsbridge Quay in 2015. (author's collection)

cavalry. Horses pulled supply wagons; they hauled the guns of the artillery and they were used to move the wounded back from the front line dressing stations.

Of course the cavalry needed horses too, but their mounts were carefully selected and well trained. Infantry and artillery officers above the rank of captain would also be mounted; and then there was the Royal Horse Artillery whose light guns could be moved swiftly around a battlefield in support of cavalry – pulled by horses. Horses have to eat and their fodder needed to be carried around – on wagons hauled by horses.

The rapid mobilisation of 1914 and the burgeoning size of the army afterwards, necessitated enormous numbers of extra horses. Military requisition teams were sent into the countryside to obtain horses for the army and South Devon was a prime contributor. Horses were requisitioned from farmers, wholesalers, brewers and retailers across the area.

Without a doubt local business was affected, at least temporarily. There are accounts of deliveries of goods being temporarily suspended during August and September 1914. With a harvest fast approaching, August was not a good time to take horses away from farmers. Ironically however, the requisitioning of its horses may have actually accelerated the mechanisation of South Devon's agriculture in the longer term.

These photographs of horses on Kingsbridge Quay on pages 18 and 20 are stored at the Cookworthy Museum, Kingsbridge and with them is a hand written account by J. Pearce of 8 Fore Street, Kingsbridge. It reads:

'Scene on Kingsbridge Quay on August 6th 1914 when between 800 and 900 horses were brought for the inspection of Army Authorities on the declaration of war by England on Germany. A large number were purchased. Never were there such a number of horses seen in Kingsbridge within living memory, extending in double lines up to the end of Ilbert Road, down the Quay, to the end of the Promenade and up to

Horses for sale on Kingsbridge Quay 1914. (Cookworthy Museum, Kingsbridge)

Kingsbridge Quay 2015. The church and buildings at the end of Fore Street can be clearly seen, but the water has been filled in to make a car park. (Author's collection)

Market Place. Horses of every description. Carriage horses, hunters, hacks, light and heavy. It being early closing day, shops were shut and everybody turned out to see such a sight. I saw 56 splendid animals being entrained at Kingsbridge Station (destined) for Bulford Camp and Salisbury Plain, to be trained for heavy Field Artillery before being sent to the Continent.'

At a distance of over a hundred years, it is easy to assume that in 1914 everyone was pulling together in an effort to win the war quickly. Not so. Sometimes, local folk turned to devious ways in order to hold on to their animals. For example, the Stowford Mill archives record that prior to a visit by a military requisition team a worker was instructed to take one of the 'best stallions' and hide it near the railway viaduct.

Furthermore, rogues and ne'er-do-wells sought to take advantage of an already bad situation. In August 1914 the *South Devon and Kingsbridge Gazette* published a warning which came from South Wales of men masquerading as War Office officials purchasing horses at knock-down prices. In one instance, these bogus officials had bought horses for £30 each and sold them on for £50.

At the beginning of the war the cavalry was a major consumer of horses. As the war progressed, however, cavalry regiments became dismounted and so the need for cavalry mounts decreased. On the other hand, and to counterbalance this, the need to supply vastly increased numbers of infantry and the growth of the artillery necessitated more and more horses for the army. The internal combustion engine was destined to replace horses in all but the ceremonial needs of the army. By the end of the conflict, however, very little had actually happened in the development of tanks, lorries and personnel carriers. From the outbreak of hostilities to the Armistice of November 1918, the horse was absolutely essential to the military of all combatant nations.

By 1915 the German navy, especially its U-boats, were proving effective in limiting Britain's supply of food by sea. At the start of

Eventually, the stock of horses in the countryside was rebuilt as this photograph of a Land Girl who helped Mr Quantick on his farm near Totnes shows. (Totnes Image Bank)

the war Britain produced just 35% of its food and it became clear that the country had to become more self-sufficient in food. Moreover, many of the men who would normally have worked on the farms had enlisted; it has been estimated that by January 1915 over 100,000 British men who worked on the land had gone to war.

Women were encouraged onto the land. There were initial reservations, especially from farmers who believed women could not do the heavier work traditionally undertaken by men. Women proved that, given proper training, they could indeed carry out the work necessary. Towards the end of 1917 there were over a quarter of a million women working as farm labourers, though only 23,000 were actually Land Girls.

The Women's Land Army was not formed until March 1917, when the Board of Agriculture established a civilian women's labour force of mobile workers. It recruited, trained for four weeks and then channelled healthy young women over 18 years of age into farm work. These Land Girls took on the task of producing the nation's food: milking, caring for livestock and general work on farms. Land Girls were paid 18 shillings a week, increasing to £1 a week after they passed an efficiency test.

Families at war

Families were bound together and torn apart by the Great War. It seemed to touch every single person in the country and, like the great plagues of previous centuries, the war threatened all – nobody was immune.

Families of all social divisions were affected. Francis Bingham Mildmay was the local MP. Born in 1861 and educated at Eton and Trinity College, Cambridge, he became a partner in a London based merchant bank. In 1885 Mildmay was elected Member of

Agricultural workers at Aveton Gifford 1917, including Granny Weekes, Mrs Mary Moore, Mrs George Adams, Mrs Jack Wyatt, Edie Elliott, Janie Steere, B. Browse and Mrs Dobell. (Cookworthy Museum, Kingsbridge)

Parliament for the Totes division, originally as a Liberal but from 1912 he sat as a Conservative. He held the seat for thirty-seven years until he retired from the Commons in 1922.

As a volunteer in the Queen's Own West Kent Yeomanry, Mildmay saw service as a major in 1900 during the Second Boer War and was quick to return to fighting in the Great War. Major Mildmay was in Flanders in 1914/15 but sent home in March 1915 for dental treatment, during which time he attended Parliament. Later he was divisional interpreter for General Sir Thomas D'Oyly Snow, who referred to Mildmay's tireless work and bravery carrying despatches around the battlefield at the Second Battle of Ypres (April/May 1915) and recommended him for a medal.

After the war Mildmay was created Baron Mildmay of Flete and was appointed Lord Lieutenant of Devon in 1928. Flete, a large country estate and house between Modbury and Plymouth built by Mildmay's father, still exists. During the war it housed a private hospital with ten beds, established by Mrs Mildmay, who went on to become the Vice President of the Totnes Division of the British Red Cross Society.

A visitor to the village of Holbeton will likely stumble upon the Mildmay Colours Inn. This pub was renamed the Mildmay Colours in the 1960s in honour of the late Lord Anthony Mildmay, an amateur jockey. His Grand National racing colours are on display.

At the other end of the social spectrum, John Higman had been the station master at Ivybridge. His son Thomas served in the 13th Gloucesters. Just down the road from Ivybridge railway station was the Chantry, the grand house where the Hawker family lived and where Florence Higman worked as a cook. Both Thomas Higman and the Hawker's son, Reggie, were killed.

A number of families lost more than one son in the war. Stephen and Constance Hammick, of St Stephen's, Plympton, lost two sons. Second Lieutenant Ernest Lumley Hammick, 1st Battalion, 73rd Carnatic Infantry died on 16 May 1916 and is buried in India. The 73rd Carnatic was an infantry regiment of the British Indian Army. Throughout the Great War the regiment was posted in India on training and internal security duties. The other son, Captain Eustace Hammick MC, was born in Torquay and commissioned into the 17th Indian Infantry (The Loyal Regiment). He died on 8 October 1918, aged 29, having been awarded both the Military Cross and the Chevalier of the Order of the Crown of Belgium. The *London Gazette* citation records his conspicuous gallantry and devotion to duty when he commanded the advanced guard in an attack on enemy positions on 18 – 20 September 1918. Although severely wounded he remained with his company until too weak to carry on.

For reasons which may only be imagined, some families seemed to become competitive in making public the numbers of their menfolk who were in the services, details being regularly published in the newspapers. For example, in November 1915 the *Kingsbridge and South Devon Gazette* reported that a Mr Dyer of West Buckland had received a letter from King George V congratulating him on having five sons in the forces. A few months later it was

Captain Reginald Sydlow Hawker, the Royal 1st Devon Yeomanry/ Machine Gun Corps. Captain Hawker wears the frock coat of the Royal 1st Devons. (unknown)

reported that a family in Sherford had six sons in the forces. Not to be outdone by this, in December the newspaper carried the story of a South Milton man who had no less than three sons, three sons-in law and seven grandsons in the services. Sadly, later on in the war the deaths of these men began to be reported.

A Kingsbridge family lost two sons at the battle of Jutland in 1916, the greatest naval battle of the war. Able Seaman Percival Charles Ferris (HMS *Defence*) and his brother Able Seaman John

Langley Ferris (HMS *Indefatigable*), the sons of Lewis and Eliza Ferris of Kingsbridge, were both killed.

William and Sibillia Hannaford lived at 3 Crescent Road in Ivybridge. They were neighbours of the Higmans and Hawkers, living just along from the Station Cottages and up above Chantry, though they probably had little direct dealings with the latter. In the spring of 1918 Mr and Mrs Hannaford received the devastating news that two of their sons had died. Albert Hannaford volunteered to serve in the Duke of Cornwall's Light Infantry, following his elder brother William, who joined the Royal Warwickshire Regiment.

On 17 April Albert was killed in France whilst fighting with the 1/5th Duke of Cornwall's Light Infantry. He was aged just 19. Two days later, on 19 April, William, aged 25 and a sergeant in the 10th Battalion of the Royal Warwickshire Regiment, was killed in Belgium. Almost to add insult to Mr and Mrs Hannaford's injuries – and to those of William's wife, Olive – neither of the Hannaford boys has a known grave; Albert is commemorated on the Loos memorial, Pas de Calais, and William on the Tyne Cot Memorial, Zonnebeke.

There were many constant reminders of the war. Next of kin were informed directly when a relative died. The newspapers and parish magazines reported the dead and the injured widely. For example, the Ivybridge Parish Magazine of June 1915 had much to report: Ernest Hoskin and Eliza Bovey had married; Annie Kitson had died aged 80; the Sick and Poor Fund held a balance of £17 1s 1/2d, and another nine young men had joined up. These were Henry Hall, John Sherrill, John Damerell, Albert West, James Bond, Sydney Exworthy, the twins Frank and Rupert Downing and John Frederick.

The magazine also informed parishioners that a former resident of Ivybridge, Sergeant Hall of the Royal Marine Light Infantry, had been killed on active service.

Later, in April 1918, the same publication reported on the death and funeral of Major John Bayly, a sidesman of St John's, Ivybridge. In his eulogy the vicar said:

'his loss would be felt throughout the county, his interest being so wide and diverse... He was a loyal, staunch fellow-Churchman, one who loved his Lord and therefore loved His Church. He was indeed a 'good' man... During the time he held office (as Sidesman) he was most generous in support of the Church Expenses. (Mr and Mrs Bayly's) beautiful screen was a lasting memorial to him and his generosity.'

No doubt all those present were moved. The screen is still there in St John's.

The story of the Grey-Smith family takes the reader far away from South Devon and discussion of the research in this case illustrates some of the issues facing the local military historian.

Amongst the fallen listed on the Bovey Tracey war memorial is Lieutenant Commander J.E. Grey-Smith, RN. The rank of lieutenant commander in the navy is broadly equivalent to a major in the army. As relatively few of the lieutenant commanders killed during the Great War are likely to have been called Grey-Smith a search of the Commonwealth War Graves Commission (CWGC) website was an obvious place to begin. This is often the best place to start, as sometimes the website contains other useful information about the deceased serviceman's family. There were also the initials J.E. to aid the search.

Nothing on the CWGC website matched the search criteria so the next step was to shorten the doubled barrelled surname to Smith.

Success! A search of the website for J.E. Smiths in the Royal Navy resulted in two outcomes. The first was a midshipman who died in 1919 whilst serving on HMS *Royal Oak*. The second was Lieutenant Commander John Essex Grey Smith (without the hyphen) who died on 17 March 1917 whilst serving on HMS *Cambrian*. He was aged 30. Moreover, the documents on the website state that he accidentally drowned and there is no known grave. Now there were two routes to forward the research: the ship and the family.

HMS *Cambrian*, according to the two websites consulted (WorldNavalShips.com and Wikipedia), was a C-class light cruiser launched in March 1916 and sold for scrap in 1934. At the time of Lieutenant Commander Grey Smith's death, she was serving with the 4th Light Cruiser Squadron, but no further details of the action in March 1917 were found.

Helpfully, the CWGC website contains some family details. His parents are listed as William Belcher Grey Smith and Dora Josephine Smith. This seems to confirm the use of Grey Smith (not Grey-Smith) as a family name, and suggests that a mistake may have been made on the Bovey Tracey war memorial. Mistakes of this kind are not, in themselves, so unusual, but this one does pose the question as to why family members in Bovey Tracey did not notice the mistake and have it corrected?

The most obvious answer is that perhaps there weren't any Grey Smiths still living in Bovey to intervene at the time the memorial was installed.

This leads to the most mystifying part of the story: according to the CWGC website Mr and Mrs Grey Smith lived at 454 Collins Street, Melbourne. The Grey Smiths were Australians.

The next step in the research was to investigate Grey Smiths not in Bovey Tracey, but in Australia. The Australian Directory of Biography lists a Francis Grey Smith (1827-1900) who was born in Cambridge, England. The family migrated to Australia in 1839 and in 1849 Francis married Susanna Amelia Belcher (daughter of a Dublin solicitor, Joseph William Belcher). This information makes a link between the three names Belcher, Grey and Smith. Following their marriage, Francis and Susanna Grey Smith went forth and multiplied. They had eight sons and three daughters. Francis had a successful career as a banker. He was also a sportsman and had a grandstand at the Melbourne Cricket Ground named after him.

Further research reveals a complex family history welded by art, sport and war. Three of the sons traced are of especial interest:

First was William Belcher Grey Smith, the father of Lieutenant Commander J.E. Grey Smith.

Second, George Frederick Belcher Grey-Smith (and here is the first reference to the hyphenated version of the family name) was the brother of William Belcher and the father of Melville Grey-Smith, Lieutenant Commander Grey Smith's cousin. Captain Melville Grey-Smith was killed in what is now Israel/Palestine on 19 November 1917. He was serving with the 2nd Battalion, 3rd Queen Alexandra's Own Gurkha Rifles.

The third son, Francis Grey-Smith married Sibylla Ann Ross. Their son Ross Grey-Smith (1901–1973) was a sportsman like his grandfather. He spent ten years at the Melbourne Church of England Grammar School because of his value as an oarsman, was Captain of Boats in 1920-21 and remained at the school until he was 20. Ross Grey-Smith became a solicitor in 1926, but found time for sport. He was a member of the Commonwealth Golf Club's pennant team in 1922 and was accomplished at tennis and shooting. Later he took to more expensive hobbies, including aviation, and was a committee-member (1931-32) of the Royal Victorian Aero Club. During the Second World War he served in the Air Force. After the war Ross was involved in horse racing, became chairman of the Victoria Racing Club and was knighted in 1966. He died without issue in 1973.

Pursuing yet another line of the Grey-Smith dynasty reveals further interesting family history and perhaps the most famous of the Grey-Smith line. One of Lieutenant Commander Grey Smith's cousins (sharing the same grandfather) was Francis Edward Grey-Smith. He married Ada Janet King and lived in Western Australia. They had three sons – Jack, Guy and Keith – all of whom served in the Australian armed forces, in the Second World War.

Private Jack Grey-Smith died in 1941, aged 23, and his younger brother Corporal Keith Grey-Smith was killed the year after, aged 22. Both of them served in the Australian Infantry force. The third brother, Guy Edward was born in 1916, joined the Royal Australian Air Force on 20 January 1936 and trained as a pilot.

In 1937 Guy took a short-service commission in the Royal Air Force and moved to England. He married Helen Stanes in October

1939, just after the outbreak of war and before being posted to France with 139 Squadron, RAF. In May 1940, during the rapidly changing events which led to the British retreat from Dunkirk, Guy Grey-Smith's Bristol Blenheim light bomber was shot down over enemy held territory in the Netherlands. He successfully baled-out, but was hit on the head by the aircraft's tail-plane and suffered severe head injuries. Guy was captured and made a German prisoner of war, held at the Stalag Luft III camp in Sagan, Poland, where he developed tuberculosis. In 1944 he returned to the UK on a prisoner exchange.

Guy had begun to sketch, using materials supplied by his wife, whilst a PoW. In 1944 he was admitted to a sanatorium at Midhurst, Sussex, where his interest in painting was further stimulated by an art therapy programme. After the war he studied under Ceri Richards and Henry Moore at the Chelsea School of Art.

In 1947 Guy relinquished his RAF commission and returned to Australia in 1948. In 1950 he and his wife renovated a house in the hills above Perth, Western Australia, where he also built a studio. Strongly influenced by the French post-Impressionist painter Paul Cézanne, Guy Grey-Smith produced some of the most emotive paintings of the Western Australian landscape. He formed the 'Perth Group' of artists in the late 1950s and was also a successful printmaker and ceramicist.

Guy Grey-Smith became a Knight of the Order of Australia in 1981, but died in August of the same year from a recurrence of the tuberculosis that had plagued him since the war. He was aged 65 and has been described as one of Australia's most significant artists.

So ends the story of the Grey-Smiths and of Lieutenant Commander J.E. Grey-Smith, RN, in particular. There is one powerful question left unanswered. Just what was the link between Lieutenant Commander John Essex Grey Smith and Bovey Tracey, on whose war memorial his name is engraved? It is clear the family were well established in Australia by 1914 so why, and at what point, did he move to this small Devon town leaving his parents and extended family?

PART 2

The Soldiers' War

Tales of local men fighting and surviving the war, and of their regiments, is important to the story of South Devon in the Great War. Not least because the local regiments, by whatever standards one might judge such things, acquitted themselves very well throughout. Two Victoria Crosses were awarded to men of the Devonshire Regiment, as was the French decoration, the *Croix de Guerre*, alongside numerous other medals. These are discussed below.

Before delving into these tales, a few words of essential information for readers not expert in military history. In the British Army, the infantry was and is organised by regiment – but it is deployed and it fights by battalion. A peacetime regiment might have two or three battalions (each of about 1,000 men commanded by a lieutenant colonel) but they would rarely serve together. A brigade (commanded by a brigadier general) comprised four battalions in 1914, cut to three later in the war, and would usually be made up of battalions from different regiments. In 1914 for example, 2 Infantry Brigade was formed of the 2nd Battalion, the Royal Sussex Regiment, the 1st Battalion, the Loyal Regiment, the 1st Battalion, the Northamptonshire Regiment and the 2nd Battalion, the King's Royal Rifle Corps.

As the war progressed and more soldiers were needed, the number of battalions in each regiment burgeoned. For example, by

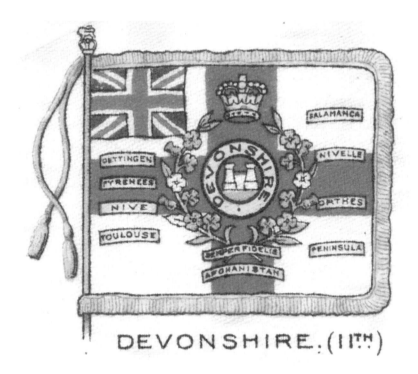

Silk postcard showing the colours of the Devonshire Regiment. Embroidered postcards from the Great War are generally known as 'WW1 Silks'. They were first produced in 1914 and declined substantially from 1918 onwards, and there are none after 1923. The silks were generally hand embroidered on strips of silk mesh with as many as twenty-five on a strip, mostly produced by French and Belgian women refugees who worked in their homes and refugee camps. (Author's collection)

1918 the Devonshire Regiment numbered twenty-four battalions (approximately 24,000 men).

In this book, the reader will be referred in the main to battalions of men, noted in the following standard form: 1st Devons (i.e. the 1st Battalion, the Devonshire Regiment) or 10th King's Own (i.e. the 10th Battalion, the King's Own Royal Lancaster Regiment. Just occasionally, mention is made of companies (four per battalion –

each commanded by a major or a captain) and platoons (four per company – each under the command of a lieutenant).

It has been suggested that there were two British armies fighting in the Great War: the Old Army and Kitchener's New Army. It may well be that tales of the 'Kitchener' infantry battalions of New Army dominate the popular imagination. This has been bolstered over the years by many tales, both brave and tragic, such as that of the decimation of the 'Accrington Pals' (11th Battalion, East Lancashire Regiment), the 'Grimsby Chums' (10th Battalion, the Lincolnshire Regiment) or the Ulster Division on the Somme battlefield in 1916. Not all 'Pals' battalions were geographically constituted. For example, there were various sportsmen's battalions in a number of regiments such as the Middlesex Regiment, the Royal Fusiliers and the Royal Scots.

The late historian Richard Holmes has strongly argued, however, that there was not one British Army in the Great War, nor two even, but four: the Old Army, the Territorial Army (then known as Territorial Force), the New Army and the Conscripted Army. It is Holmes's structure that gives shape to what follows in this chapter.

Before proceeding to examine the work of the local regiments, however, mention must be made of the fact that men from South Devon served in every branch of the army and at all ranks.

Private Robert Luscombe, 6th (City of London) Battalion, the London Regiment who was born in Blackawton, grew up in Kingsbridge and later moved to London. He died on 1 July 1917 aged 24.

Private Frank Lewis Bovey the son of William and Selina Bovey, Kingsteignton served with the Army Veterinary Corps at the 31st Veterinary Hospital in what is now Palestine. He died of dysentery on 21 August 1918.

Private (Acting Corporal) John Reginald Gilley, 1st Battalion Coldstream Guards, who was the son of Mr and Mrs John Gilley of Bovey Tracey, died on 27 September 1918 in France.

Corporal Francis (Frank) William Voysey, 32nd Motor Ambulance Convoy, Royal Army Medical Corps, was the son of

Francis and Ellen Voysey of Kingsbridge and brother of Mrs Annie Harris, of Paignton. He died on 5 September 1918 aged 27.

Lance Sergeant Richard John Percival (Percy) Oldrieve, 1st Battalion, the Coldstream Guards, died on 13 November 1914 aged 26. He was the son of Richard and Augustina Oldrieve of Dartmouth.

Company Sergeant Major Victor Maddicott, 16th Battalion, the Devonshire Regiment, who died on 10 September 1918, aged 28, was the son of Mr and Mrs Maddicott of Heathfield.

Second Lieutenant Reginald P.O. Weekes, 10 Squadron Royal Flying Corps, was the son of Reginald Newton and Ida Mousell Weekes of Modbury. He was born in Brixham and killed in action on 7 May 1917 aged 19.

Captain Cecil Aubrey Bradford, Yorkshire Regiment, attached to the Nigeria Regiment, Royal West African Frontier Force was drowned on 24 April 1917, aged 31. He was the second son of the late Lieutenant Colonel O.J. Bradford, of Welparke, Lustleigh.

Major Hubert Symons, Royal Field Artillery (D Battery, 47th Brigade) who died on 22 March 1918, aged 32, was the husband of Mary Beatrice Erskine Symons of Bovey Tracey.

Perhaps the most famous of South Devon's soldiers was Major (acting lieutenant colonel) Herbert Cecil Buller DSO. Buller was the son of the late Admiral Sir Alexander Buller GCB and Lady Buller of Plympton. He joined the regular army in 1900 and was commissioned into the Rifle Brigade. Upon the outbreak of war Buller was one of three British regular officers appointed to the Princess Patricia's Canadian Light Infantry (Eastern Ontario Regiment). The regiment was named after Princess Patricia of Connaught, a granddaughter of Queen Victoria, and was affectionately known at the time as the Princess Pat's. It recruited British ex-pats in Canada. Buller initially served as adjutant to oversee the critical process of recruiting, but following the death of the commanding officer Colonel Farquhar at St Eloi, Buller assumed command of the regiment and led it from 21 March 1915 to 4 May 1915 when he was wounded at the Battle of Ypres – losing an eye. He recovered from injury and commanded the Princess Pat's a second time from 7 December 1915 to 2 June 1916. Buller was awarded the Distinguished Service Order for his action during the Second Battle of Ypres and was twice mentioned in despatches. He was killed in action on 3 June 1916, aged 34.

Colonel Frank Ridley Farrer Boileau, Royal Engineers was attached to the General Staff in France, where he died of wounds on 28 August 1914, aged 46. He was the son of Colonel F.W. Boileau CB and Letitia Boileau (née Bradford) of Lustleigh, and the husband of Mary A. Boileau, of Windout Hill House, Exeter.

The Old Army

The Army reforms of 1908, brought about by Secretary of State for War, Richard Haldane, and known therefore as the Haldane Reforms, dictated that each infantry regiment should comprise two regular battalions and a reserve battalion supported by a number of Territorial Force battalions.

Before 1914 men who wished to join the army as a career had the choice of regiment. Many chose to join the local battalions, if they would have them, but there are a number of factors that complicate regimental regional affiliation. Personal reasons may have led men to request service in particular units. For example, Private Bentley Moore of Totnes found himself in the London Scottish Regiment in 1914, and the Ivybridge parish magazine of June 1915 (well before conscription) informs us that 'Walter Williams, 1st Leinster Regiment, has been wounded, but is mending'. Private Percy George Brimblecombe from Chagford was formerly a Territorial with the Devon Yeomanry, but served with the 9th Battalion, the Cheshire Regiment. He was killed in action on 31 May 1918.

Sometimes men with a local connection had moved away by 1914 and, naturally enough, decided to join units closer to where they resided. If their families remained in South Devon, however, they may well be commemorated on one of the local memorials. One such was Kingdon Tregosse Frost who is commemorated on the war memorial in Bovey Tracey and in the local church. He was also one of the first local men to die in the war. Frost served as a lieutenant in the 3rd (Special Reserve) Battalion, the Cheshire Regiment and was attached to the 1st Cheshires when war broke out. He was killed at Mons on 28 August 1914 aged 37. His is a story of valour in the field and an unknown grave.

Kingdon Tregosse Frost was born on 12 March 1877 in Launceston, Cornwall. His parents were Denis Tregosse and Sophia Margaret Frost; his father was a solicitor. Kingdon Frost's two brothers also held commissions during the Great War. One was Captain Russell Tregosse Frost, who also served with the Cheshire Regiment. The younger brother, Oswald Milles Tregosse Frost, was a major in the Dorset Regiment during the Great War and went on to become a lieutenant colonel. In 1941 he wrote the army reference book, *Vade-Mecum for Field-General Courts-Martial*. Oswald Frost died in 1943 and is buried locally, in Chudleigh.

Kingdon Frost was educated at Bath School, Brasenose College, Oxford and the British school at Athens (from 1902 to 1904) from where he also spent some time in Egypt. In 1904 he returned to England, briefly taking up a post at Isleworth Training College and was elected a Fellow of the Royal Geographical Society in 1905. Then it was back to Egypt for a second time where he worked for the Ministry of Education between 1905 and 1908 before returning to England, working in the Bodleian Library, Oxford, from 1908 to 1909. From 1909 up to the declaration of war in 1914, Kingdon Frost was lecturer in Archaeology and Ancient History at Queen's University, Belfast, being the first archaeology lecturer there.

At Queen's he was a member of the Officer Training Corps and in September 1912 he joined the 3rd (Special Reserve) Battalion of the Cheshire Regiment. He was commissioned the following year.

When the 1st Cheshires went into battle on the second day of the Battle of Mons, in addition to their regular officers they took with them six officers from the Special Reserve, Frost included. By 6pm that night, three 1st Cheshire officers had been killed and fifteen captured. Only seven officers remained. Lieutenant Frost was one of those killed.

In the heat of battle, somebody reported British soldiers to the rear of Frost's platoon retiring and Frost went to identify them. The soldiers he went to check on turned out to be Germans, and it is from their accounts that details of Frost's fate surfaced. The German accounts said that Frost 'fought like a demon and refused to surrender although wounded several times'. He refused to give in, the Germans reported, and 'death alone overcame his indomitable spirit'. Later, back in Bovey Tracey, Lieutenant Frost's family had clearly received details of this description of his death. They had a memorial to him placed in the Parish Church of St Peter, St Paul and St Thomas and it records that although 'isolated he refused quarter and fell fighting'.

The Germans buried Lieutenant Frost with full military honours and they marked his grave with a simple wooden cross. It seems, however, that the cross bearing his name was lost by the end of the war when the Commonwealth War Graves Commission took over the cemeteries. The CWGC erected an unmarked Portland stone

Memorial to Lieutenant Kingdon Tregosse Frost in Parish Church of St Peter, St Paul and St Thomas, Bovey Tracey. (Author's collection)

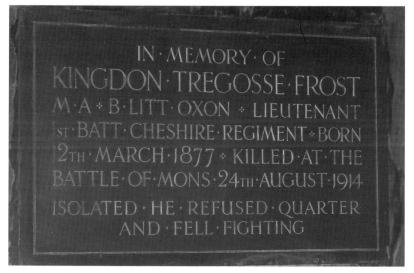

IN · MEMORY · OF
KINGDON · TREGOSSE · FROST
M · A ✦ B · LITT · OXON ✦ LIEUTENANT
1st · BATT · CHESHIRE · REGIMENT ✦ BORN
12th · MARCH · 1877 ✦ KILLED · AT · THE
BATTLE · OF · MONS · 24th · AUGUST · 1914
ISOLATED · HE · REFUSED · QUARTER
AND · FELL · FIGHTING

memorial in Wiheries Communal Cemetery, Belgium. For 80 years Lieutenant Frost's body lay in an unmarked grave with just the words 'A Soldier of the Great War, Unknown Officer 1914' on the headstone. In 1994, responding to investigations carried out by Mr Alan Gregson, the CWGC had a new headstone put in place. The words on the new headstone read 'believed to be Lieutenant Kingdon Tregosse Frost, the Cheshire Regiment'.

Private Barter, allegedly the tallest soldier in the British Army during the Great War became a Guardsman. Barter stood 6 feet 8½ inches tall. Given his height it is perhaps no surprise that he was taken on by the Grenadier Guards. The name of the bugler in the photo remains elusive, but we can still appreciate the wit of the photographer. When he was wounded in the right shoulder by a German bullet, no hospital

Private H. Barter, Grenadier Guards. The photograph was taken in 1900 when Barter was aged 18. (Totnes Image Bank)

bed was long enough for Barter and so a special bed had to be constructed for him. Rather ironic, then, that he hailed from the very small village of Littlehempston, near Totnes.

Another example of a pre-war career soldier is Robert Orlebar of Ivybridge. He was the son of Colonel and Mrs Orlebar of Rutt House. Robert was born into a military family in Walmer, Kent, his father being an officer in the Royal Marine Light Infantry. Like his father, Robert planned to be a career soldier. After graduating from Sandhurst in October 1913, he was commissioned into the Middlesex Regiment.

At the outbreak of war Robert was serving as a platoon commander with the 2nd Middlesex in Malta. The battalion returned to England in September and moved to Hursley Park, Hampshire. They were attached to 23 Infantry Brigade, formed by bringing together regular army units which had been stationed at various points around the British Empire. Coincidentally, the 2nd Devons was also part of this brigade.

In November 1914 the brigade moved to France, where the British Expeditionary Force badly needed reinforcement, landing at Le Havre on 7 November. The first major engagement for the 2nd Middlesex was the battle of Neuve Chapelle, March – April 1915. But by then Robert was dead, shot by a German

Lieutenant Robert Evelyn Orlebar 2nd Battalion, The Middlesex Regiment. (unknown)

sniper on 9 January. He was 20 years old and is buried in Rue-du-Bacquerot No.1 Cemetery, Laventie, France. As well as having his name engraved on the Ivybridge war memorial and at the Royal Military Academy, Sandhurst, there is a private family memorial in St John's Church, Ivybridge.

The fact remains, however, that before the war and until conscription was introduced in 1916, most men enlisted into their local regiments. Whether these men from South Devon were army reservists, had long desired to become soldiers or they had simply enlisted in response to public hyperbole or out of a sense of duty mattered little. In all of these cases the local regiments were the obvious places to go. The local regiments were the Devonshire Regiment, and to a lesser extent the Royal Marine Light Infantry and the Duke of Cornwall's Light Infantry.

The Regular Battalions of the Bloody Eleventh
The county regiment was originally the 11th (North Devonshire) Regiment of Foot, nicknamed the Bloody Eleventh following its losses in the Battle of Salamanca, during the Peninsular War against

Napoleon. At the outbreak of the Great War the Devonshire Regiment comprised two regular battalions – both of which were overseas in August 1914 – and the 3rd (Special Reserve) Battalion, which was essentially a training unit. It will be helpful now to consider each of these battalions in order.

The 1st Battalion, the Devonshire Regiment

The 1st Devons had been in Jersey since September 1909 and when the 'warning order' for mobilisation came on 29 July 1914, the battalion's strength stood at 450 qualified for active service. Of these, however, three officers and fifteen NCOs were sent almost immediately to Exeter to form the nucleus of a new service battalion (the 7th Devons, see below).

The battalion landed at Le Havre in late August 1914 whereupon its reservists – comprising seven officers and 633 other ranks – joined the rest, bringing it up to full strength. The 1st Devons spent Christmas 1914 in Wulverghem, Belgium, and the battalion diary records nine men killed and two wounded on Christmas Eve, two men wounded on Christmas Day – which tells something about the 1914 Christmas truce.

Apart from a brief period of 1917/18 when it was sent to Italy, the 1st Devons fought the whole of the Great War on the Western Front. Private Bertram Louis Walke may have been typical of the local men who were regulars in the 1st Battalion. Having been wounded previously, Private Walke received a bullet wound in the head and died on 11 June 1918 in a French hospital. His father, Thomas, died in 1924 but his mother, Treffina Walke, lived to the ripe old age of 95; both are buried in Ivybridge cemetery.

Lance Corporal George Onions VC

One of the soldiers of the 1st Devons decorated for valour was George Onions who had a somewhat chequered army career. He was from the Midlands and enlisted into the 3rd (King's Own) Hussars on 5 September 1914. He was later commissioned for a short period in an unknown regiment, but had to relinquish his

George Onions later in life, wearing his Victoria Cross ribbon on a captain's uniform. (The Keep Military Museum, Dorchester)

commission as a result of an altercation with an assistant provost marshal.

Onions then went to France, but served in the 9th Reserve Cavalry Regiment during the Easter Rising of 1916 in Ireland. From the Reserve Cavalry, Onions transferred to the Devonshire Regiment on 14 April 1917. On 22 August 1918, south of Achiet-le-Petit in France, the 1st Devons were in new positions gained only the day before. Lance Corporal Onions and Private Henry Eades were sent out to make contact with the battalion on the 1st Devons' right flank. Onions observed the enemy advancing in large numbers to counter-attack, and this is what the *London Gazette* had to say about what happened next:

> *'Realising his opportunity, he boldly placed himself with his comrade (Private Eades) on the flank of the advancing enemy and opened rapid fire when the target was most favourable. When the enemy were about 100 yards from him, the line wavered and some hands were seen to be thrown up. Lance Corporal Onions then rushed forward and, with the assistance of his comrade, took about 200 of the enemy prisoners and marched them back to his company commander. By his magnificent courage and presence of mind, he averted what might have been a very dangerous situation.'*

George Onions received the Victoria Cross for most conspicuous bravery and initiative; Eades received the Distinguished Conduct Medal. Onion's VC was presented by the King at Buckingham Palace on 13 February 1919. Immediately following the presentation, Onions was commissioned for a second time, this time to the Rifle Brigade in recognition of his valuable services. This commission lasted for one day only and Onions was demobilized the next day, 14 February 1919. The army commission probably boosted his pension and he was allowed to wear the uniform of the Rifle Brigade on appropriate occasions. After the war, George Onions served in the notorious Auxiliary Division of the Royal Irish Constabulary, and as an army officer of the Home Guard during the Second World War. He died in April 1944.

The 2nd Battalion, the Devonshire Regiment
The 2nd Devons had been in Egypt since January 1912. When war was declared in August the commanding officer was in Cyprus and several officers were on leave in England. On 14 September the battalion embarked on the SS *Osmanieh* at Cairo and sailed to Southampton, arriving early in October. They picked up 273 reservists at Hursley Park, near Winchester, which brought the battalion's

strength to 29 officers and 938 other ranks. However, the 2nd Devons then lost a number of warrant officers and NCOs to commissions. For example, Sergeant Chandler was commissioned and posted to the 1st Suffolks (presumably as a lieutenant, but possibly as a captain) and he went on to command that battalion in the last six months of the war.

The 2nd Devons sailed to France and were in action in late 1914, attacking a strongpoint known as the Moated Grange and suffering 130 casualties in so doing.

The battalion diary for Christmas Day 1914 records an 'informal armistice during daylight. Germans got out of their trenches and came towards our lines. Our men met them and they wished each other a Merry Xmas. Shook hands, exchanged smokes, etc. About 7.30pm sniping began again. We had one man killed one wounded,' at this time the 2nd Devons were in trenches near Neuve Chapelle and Private Arthur Horton of Ivybridge was with them.

Arthur was the son of Phillip and Elizabeth Horton. He was born in Plymouth, but in 1915 his parents lived at 11 Belmont Road, Ivybridge. Arthur was a regular soldier. The 1911 census lists him as aged 21 and serving overseas (Egypt) with the 2nd Devons.

In 1915 the battalion was heavily involved in Battle of Neuve Chapelle, fought between 10 and 13 March. This was part of an Allied offensive in the Artois region of France, and 40,000 British and Indian soldiers took part in the attack. The British broke through the German defences, but were unable to exploit their success. They suffered appalling casualties: 7,000 British and 4,200 Indian troops were killed, wounded or missing.

Arthur Horton was one of those killed as a result of the fighting at Neuve Chapelle. He died on 12 March, aged 25, and is buried in Boulogne Eastern Cemetery, France. Boulogne being about 50 miles from the fighting and with a British military hospital there, it can be inferred that Private Horton was wounded and died of those wounds in the hospital.

Two months of relative quiet followed Neuve Chappelle. Throughout April reinforcements arrived to replace casualties, but by the beginning of May the battalion was still under-strength and was particularly short of officers. William Northcott of Ivybridge was with the battalion by then; he was aged 21.

Sometimes it is difficult for the historian to establish just where and how a serviceman died, and Private Northcott is such an example. From the available evidence it is far from clear what happened to him.

First, a list of what is known. The 2nd Devons were involved in the attack on Aubers Ridge on 9 May and suffered tremendous casualties: 67 soldiers were killed or missing and 167 – including the commanding officer, Colonel Ingles – were wounded.

Private 9639 Northcott, W. died on 25 May and was buried in Rue-Petillon Military Cemetery, Fleurbaix, northern France, about four kilometres north of Aubers.

One possibility is that William Northcott may have been wounded during the attack on Aubers Ridge and then died and was buried (or, more likely, re-buried as after the war many graves in the area were concentrated on the Rue-Petillon cemetery.) However, this is unlikely for two reasons. First, there were sixteen days between the attack on Aubers Ridge and William's death, which is more than enough time to move a wounded soldier to a hospital. Second, dressing stations, field hospitals and larger hospitals were behind the front line – which would put them west of Aubers, not north of it.

It is more likely then, that William Northcott was killed or died of wounds received after the battle. Soldiers could be killed in many ways. Snipers were always active. Northcott may have been selected – or volunteered – to take part in a night time raid. The size and shape of a British Army latrine was almost exactly the same as a trench mortar emplacement, making it the target of enemy artillery and many soldiers were killed whilst on the toilet.

It is more than likely that Private William Alfred Northcott may simply have been unlucky, in the wrong place at the wrong time. He left a widow, Elizabeth Northcott, 7 Jubilee Place, Plymouth.

The Last Stand of the 2nd Devons
Just as this book would be poorer without mention of the local

regiment, so too any text on the 2nd Devons would be incomplete without referring to the action that took place in May 1918 at the Bois de Buttes for which the battalion was awarded the French *Croix de Guerre*.

As the war continued casualties in the regular battalions were replaced by volunteers and conscripts. By mid-1915 the 1st and 2nd Battalions were not the same units of Old Contemptibles they had been in 1914. As the war dragged on the situation worsened.

The 2nd Devons had been severely depleted by the fighting of March and April 1918, as they struggled to hold back General Ludendorff's Spring Offensive. The battalion received badly needed reinforcements, some (who were fully trained) from the Devon Yeomanry, but a larger number of young soldiers who were hardly trained at all. Changes in the battalion's command also reflects shortages. On 7 April 1918 Lieutenant Colonel Rupert Anderson-Morshead took command of the 2nd Devons, with (acting) Major Cope his second in command. They were a good team, both men were well regarded by officers and men throughout the battalion. Captain U.B. Burke was the adjutant.

Anderson-Morshead originated from the small seaside town of Sidmouth in South Devon, though his home was Lingfield, Surrey. He was the son of John and Helen Anderson-Morshead. He assumed the rank of lieutenant colonel when he took command of the 2nd Devons, yet Morshead was but 32 years old and his substantive rank was still captain (he had previously been promoted to the post of temporary major). This is not to suggest that he was in any way not up to the task of commanding an infantry battalion – indeed he turned out to be extremely brave, professional and more than competent. It does illustrate, however, the high turnover of officers during the Great War.

On 12 May the 2nd Devons were attached to a French army, and sent to a 'quiet sector' to recuperate and rebuild. Lieutenant Colonel Anderson-Morshead set about training what was an almost new battalion. He soon lost Major Cope who was sent to a divisional machine-gun training school.

Unfortunately for the men of the 2nd Devons, the quiet sector they were sent to was a target of the German offensive that began on 27 May. The battalion was soon ordered to occupy positions on the Bois des Buttes, a wooded sandstone hill south-west of La Ville-aux-Bois. Positioned approximately 1,200 yards behind the front line, the 2nd Devons were to be the reserve for 23 Brigade – the 2nd West Yorkshires and 2nd Middlesex stood in front of them.

At 1am on the 27th the opening bombardment of the German attack began with shelling and poison gas. Anderson-Morshead had his men wearing their gas masks in the safety of tunnels under the hill, all except Private Giles of A Company who pleaded claustrophobia, spent the whole time of the bombardment in the open and remained unharmed.

The units of the West Yorkshire and Middlesex Regiments in the front-line trenches suffered terribly from this bombardment. When, at about 3.45am, the bombardment lifted and the German infantry attacked them they were rapidly infiltrated and overrun. The Germans advanced, using the recently developed *sturmtruppen* (stormtrooper) tactics: moving rapidly, probing for weak spots and avoiding pockets of resistance.

At this point in the battle, Anderson-Morshead ordered the 2nd Devons out of the tunnels to man the trenches. He found that his battalion was the only cohesive unit of any size in the area. Running through the 2nd Devons' trenches on the Bois des Buttes were French soldiers and wounded men from both the Middlesex and West Yorkshire regiments.

The 2nd Devons were in action as soon as they left the tunnels. By this time they were almost completely surrounded and a frantic and bitter fight followed. Every soldier of the 2nd Devons – the cooks and transport men, all the HQ including Lieutenant Colonel Anderson-Morshead and his adjutant, were fighting for their lives. In places the Germans were close enough to throw grenades; in others men of the Devonshire Regiment charged with bayonets in their attempt to see off the German attack.

The battalion was split and there was little or no communication between sections of it. Lieutenant Leat with seven or eight men of his C Company platoon remaining joined up with Lieutenant Tindal, also of C Company. Between them they mustered sixteen or eighteen soldiers. Lieutenant Tindal called together his senior ranks and told them that as he had no orders to retire he would remain in position. He divided the remnants of the company into two sections. One provided covering fire whilst the second charged the enemy. Lieutenant Tindal was later killed whilst trying to silence a German sniper.

By 7am, after some three hours of desperate fighting, the 2nd Devons had suffered enormous casualties, but they continued to harass the advancing Germans from the reverse slope of the hill. By 9am there were only about fifty or sixty men of the HQ Company still fit to fight. Anderson-Morshead, divided these into two groups and moved them from the hill down to the road to attack the Germans on two flanks. About this time, an artillery officer with a small group of unarmed men encountered Anderson-Morshead 'calmly writing his notes with a perfect hail of high explosive falling round him. . . he told me nothing could be done (and) refused all offers of help'.

There is no single coherent account of the fighting, what exists has been re-constructed from the 2nd Devons' war diaries, personal diaries and letters which are kept with the Devonshire Regiment archives at the Keep Military Museum, Dorchester. In one such letter Captain Burke (who survived the battle of the Bois des Buttes, was awarded the Military Cross and was still serving in the battalion ten years later, still as a captain) wrote the following to Lieutenant Colonel Anderson-Morshead's brother:

> *The Colonel, seeing our men keeping their heads too low, got upon our parapet and directed our fire as successive targets appeared. Our men were alright by now and our fire became very effective and caused great casualties especially in a division of German artillery coming down the road from Juveney to Roucy. . . About 11am the Colonel had gone round*

the trenches as several times before. Shortly afterwards when crossing the top of the hill, his usual route, he fell heavily forward and lay motionless. . .'

Eventually, short of ammunition and greatly outnumbered, the survivors conducted a fighting withdrawal to the River Aisne.

In all, twenty-three officers and 528 other ranks of the 2nd Devons were killed or posted as missing that morning. Between forty and eighty survivors managed to cross the Aisne and the nearby canal, and re-join the retreating British forces.

It is still unclear whether Lieutenant Colonel Anderson-Morshead had received orders to stand and fight on the Bois des Buttes. A very general order of no retreat had been urged on the British by the French (who were in overall command). Captain Burke, writing afterwards, insisted that a message from Divisional HQ came up some time after 5am ordering the battalion to 'stay put' and not retire. In any case, like his junior officer, Lieutenant Tindal, Anderson-Morshead's instinct would have been to fight on unless ordered otherwise.

The importance of the 2nd Devons' stand on 27 May cannot be underestimated. Had Morshead surrendered at 4am the most likely outcome would have been a German breakthrough. As it was, the Devons fought on until sometime after 12.30pm, allowing reserves to be deployed.

The sacrifice of the 2nd Devons was recognised by the award of the French *Croix de Guerre* with palm in December 1918, the first such award to a British regiment. The importance that the British attached to the action is indicated by the fact that the honour Bois des Buttes was included in the first of a total of ten lists of battle honours for the Great War, published in February 1924.

The 3rd (Special Reserve) Battalion

The 3rd Battalion of the Devonshire Regiment was formed in 1908 and was a training and holding unit. Days before the declaration of war, when conflict with Germany seemed inevitable, the reservists were called up – personal telegrams and/or recall notices pinned to the doors of post offices being the usual means of communication. The role of the 3rd Battalion was to receive reservists and, later, soldiers recovered from injury or illness, and prepare them for deployment to another battalion. It was based in Exeter until May 1915.

In 1915 the 3rd Devons moved to Devonport and were based at the North Raglan barracks there until the end of the war. The battalion's training function was augmented by the need for further troops to strengthen the garrison responsible for the defence of Plymouth. To this end, the Citadel in Plymouth – now the home of 12 (Commando) Royal Artillery – was garrisoned by elements of the 3rd Devons throughout the war.

The Territorial Force

The Territorial Force of the pre-war Devonshire Regiment was four battalions strong: the 4th, 5th, 6th and 7th (Cyclists) Battalions.

The 4th Battalion, The Devonshire Regiment Formed in 1908 along with the other Territorial battalions, the 4th Battalion of the Devonshire Regiment was raised from volunteers living in Exeter and East Devon. In August 1914 the 4th Battalion was undergoing its annual training camp at Woodbury along with the 5th and 6th Devons and two Territorial battalions of the Duke of Cornwall's Light Infantry. There are a number of accounts of these men

A Player's cigarette card depicting an officer of the Exeter and South Devon Volunteer Rifle Corps in 1852, in front of Exeter Castle. The jacket and trousers are in 'Rifle' green. This unit eventually became the 4th (Territorial) Battalion of the Devonshire Regiment. (Author's collection)

disembarking from trains at Exmouth railway station and marching the four miles to Woodbury Common.

The 5th (Prince of Wales's) Battalion, The Devonshire Regiment

Formed in 1908 from a merger of the 2nd (Plymouth) Battalion and the Haytor Volunteer Rifles, this battalion recruited volunteers from Plymouth and South Devon. In 1805 the 2nd Battalion had been designated the Prince of Wales's and had received Prince of Wales's colours in 1871. Until 1908 they continued to wear the green number one dress tunics of the Rifles, but reluctantly converted to red following the Haldane Reforms.

The designation Prince of Wales's was, however, retained by the 5th Devons. The battalion was commanded by Lieutenant Colonel F.K. Windeatt.

The 6th Battalion, The Devonshire Regiment

This battalion recruited volunteers from north Devon. Along with the 4th and 5th Devons it was camped on Woodbury Common in August 1914. On the declaration of war the Woodbury camp was dismantled on a bright sunny day and the 4th, 5th and 6th Devons marched into Exeter. Lance Corporal Greenslade recorded that, 'everybody turned out to cheer us as if we were the most wonderful people on the face of the earth. . . little thinking that in a few weeks we would just be the poor bloody infantry.'

The soldiers marched to Exeter's St David's station and boarded trains bound for Plymouth. There, the 1,400 soldiers of the 5th and 6th Devons were crammed into a small drill hall in Plymouth without facilities for washing or feeding.

Out of this initial chaos came order and by 9 August all three of these Territorial Force infantry battalions had moved by train to Salisbury Plain.

The 7th (Cyclist) Battalion, The Devonshire Regiment

The Cyclist Battalion was also formed in 1908 and was based in Totnes. It had completed its 1914 annual training by August and quickly mobilised and assembled in Totnes. The battalion was dispersed in detachments undertaking coast-watch duties; their mission was to guard the coast from Land's End to Lyme Regis. For example, B Company, 7th Devons was posted to Torquay on 18 January 1915 under the command of Captain Gorwyn. The men were ordered to report any signs of enemy aircraft, ships, or illegal signals made from the shore.

Later the battalion was moved to the north of England, ordered to patrol almost 100 miles of North Sea coast where their superior speed and mobility would be of the essence.

A problem that faced all of the army in 1914 and 1915 was that the Territorial volunteers had signed contracts to serve in defence of the homeland in the event of an invasion. The men were not obliged to fight overseas. Many Territorials volunteered at once to fight abroad – but others did not. This led to the ungainly 'fractional' system of numbering battalions. In this system, for example, the 1/5th commanded by Lieutenant Colonel Hawker in 1914, was available for full active service overseas, whilst the 2/5th remained for home defence. Those Territorials who did not volunteer for service overseas remained in the UK, but it should not be imagined that home defence was in any way trivial. The threat of some form of German invasion, perhaps supported by Gothas and Zeppelins, remained a possibility into 1918.

The first months of the war saw Territorial battalions posted to India and other parts of the Empire so that the regulars could be sent to fight in Belgium and France. In this way many local men glimpsed for the first time parts of the Empire or of continental Europe. Bugler William Thomas 'Bill' Gill, 1/5th Devons, was aged just fourteen in 1914 and when the battalion left for India. Bill Gill became the youngest British soldier serving overseas.

For some Territorials it was to be not only their first glimpse of Empire, but their last. For example, Cephas Hurrell – the son of Mr and Mrs Hurrell of Keaton Road, Ivybridge – volunteered to join the 1/4th Battalion, though most of the battalion was raised from volunteers living in east Devon. Private Hurrell died of malaria in

India in 1918 and is buried in the Trimulgherry Cantonment Cemetery.

Captain Gilbert Dore Vicary was the son of Octavia Vicary of Dyrons, Newton Abbot and the late Charles Gilbert Vicary. Gilbert was a member of the Newton Abbot Freemasons' Lodge and a Territorial. He died in November 1917 whilst serving with the 1/5th Devons in Deir el-Belah, in what is now Palestine.

Private William Roskelly (1/5th Battalion) died in Villers-Plouich, France in 1918. He was the son of Edith Turner of 8 Costly Street, Ivybridge.

The Yeomanry

Standing beside the Territorials was another volunteer force, the Yeomanry. This was the mounted adjunct to the regular cavalry. The Yeoman soldier needed to be wealthy as he had to provide both his horse and his uniform. It would be wrong, however, to think that all Yeomanry soldiers were either aristocrats or gentleman farmers, for the majority of them were privates – ordinary men. Any man good with horses who could ride was welcome and it would not have been unusual for a farmer or country gent to have also brought along a servant or two for military service.

A typical Yeoman officer type was Reggie Hawker who is listed in the 1911 Census as a wine merchant. He was the son of Ernest William Hawker, also a wine merchant, and lived at The Chantry, Ivybridge – a large house which is still standing on the edge of the Longtimber Woods that reach up to Dartmoor – along with his mother, his younger sister, Margaret, and four servants.

Of most importance to the South Devon story were two regiments of Yeomanry: the Royal North Devon Hussars (north being something of a misnomer in this case for although nominally a north Devon unit, its squadrons were based across the county, D Squadron had a detachment based at Roborough, near Plymouth) and the Royal 1st Devon Yeomanry. They were relatively small units, each of these Yeomanry regiments being around 500 men, roughly half the size of an infantry battalion.

The Royal North Devon Hussars was first raised in 1798 and had several names over the years such as the North Devonshire Regiment of Yeomanry Cavalry and the Royal North Devonshire Regiment of Yeomanry Cavalry. In 1868 the regiment was known as the Royal North Devon Hussars (a name which stuck) with headquarters at Barnstaple. Then in 1908 the regiment was renamed for the final time as the Royal North Devon Yeomanry and transferred to the Territorial Force, trained and equipped as hussars.

In May 1914 the Royal North Devons trained near Dulverton, Somerset for two weeks and in August it was mobilised as part of the 2nd South Western Mounted Brigade. For a couple of days its squadrons assembled and trained, then congregated at Barnstable and the regiment took a whole day to board the two trains allocated to it bound for the Colchester area.

The Royal 1st Devon Yeomanry's HQ was in Exeter and it had four squadrons spread across the southern half of Devon. In May 1914 430 of its men with their horses camped and trained at Lower Haytor Downs, near Bovey Tracey. It too was mobilised in August 1914, C Squadron attending church in Totnes prior to leaving Devon.

Due to the nature of fighting in the Great War the need for cavalry diminished; the Devon Yeomanry Regiments were dismounted in September 1915. This seems to have been too much for Captain Reggie Hawker, who volunteered to serve with the newly formed Machine Gun Corps. For some reason, many cavalry officers once dismounted volunteered for the Machine Gun Corps or the Royal Flying Corps. Perhaps these new units were perceived as more glamorous or exciting than the infantry. Sadly, Captain Reggie Hawker – the wine merchant from Ivybridge – died of wounds in Egypt in November 1917.

Meanwhile, still part of the 2nd South Western Mounted Brigade, the foot soldiers of the Royal North Devon Yeomanry were sent overseas. Gallipoli was not a solely ANZAC affair, there were many British and Indian troops sent there. There was also local involvement, for in September 1915 the 1/1st Royal North Devon

Yeomanry, boarded the troop ship RMS *Olympic* and sailed the next day for Turkey. The Devonshire men arrived at Mudras on 1 October and went on to Suvla Bay. By November they were in the firing line, but were evacuated on 19 December.

With them was John Bayly of Highlands House, Ivybridge, a major in the Royal North Devon Hussars. Major Bayly never fully recovered from the typhoid he contracted in Gallipoli. He died on 26 February 1918 aged 48 and is buried in the family plot at Sheepstor.

Herbert Cecil Algar of the Royal 1st Devon Yeomanry was a keen diarist and his writings cover the period from September 1915 to July 1918. On 25 September 1915 he recorded the regiment's departure from Liverpool, 'all aboard were in high spirits and we were escorted by three destroyers – soon saw the last of dear old England.'

They were bound for Gallipoli and soon after Herbert wrote that he and his comrades were under heavy shelling from the Turks. On 11 November 1915, Herbert wrote about the death of the 'best officer', Captain Teddy Hain from St Ives in Cornwall, which had 'cast a gloom over the whole regiment'. Captain Edward Hain was the son Sir Edward and Lady Hain, of Treloyhan, St Ives, Cornwall. He was aged 28 when he was killed in action.

In January 1917, the Royal 1st Devons and the Royal North Devon Hussars were amalgamated to form the rather cumbersomely named 16th (Royal 1st Devon and Royal North Devon Yeomanry) Battalion, Devonshire Regiment.

Yet the yeoman traditions died hard. Eighteen months after the amalgamation, Company Sergeant Major Sydney Gilbert Victor Maddicott (the son of Mr and Mrs H. Maddicott from Heathfield, near Newton Abbot) was killed. It was September 1918 and CSM Maddicott was serving in France with 16th Devons; but the war memorial in Bovey Tracey lists him as serving with the Devonshire Yeomanry. He was aged 28.

With the 74th Division, the 16th Devons took part in the invasion of Palestine in 1917. It fought in the second (April 1917) and third

(November 1917) battles of Gaza – and was involved in the capture of both Beersheba and the Sheria Position. Private Robert Henry Hannaford, born in Ivybridge – parents living in Plympton by 1917 – was killed in June, between the two battles and is buried in the Gaza War cemetery.

Herbert Algar's last diary entry was on 14 July 1918, by which time the Royal 1st Devons had become the 16th Devons, said: 'Packing to go back to France'. He survived and became a farmer after the war. Later he had an accident which paralysed his left arm, then the family moved to Plymouth where Herbert became a postman. When the diaries were returned to Herbert Algar's son, Edgar, he said that his father had never mentioned his wartime exploits to the family.

As with the 4th, 5th and 6th infantry battalions, the Yeomanry soon formed 2nd line regiments mirroring those who had volunteered to fight overseas. The 2nd line Royal North Devons was formed at Barnstaple in September 1914. In May 1915 it joined 2/2nd South Western Mounted Brigade at Woodbury. Later that year the regiment moved to Colchester, where its hussars took over the horses of the newly dismounted first line regiment. In April 1916 the regiment went to Norfolk and joined the 1st Mounted Division there. In July 1916 the 2nd Royal North Devons was converted to a cyclist unit and was based in Suffolk, patrolling the East Anglian coastline as part of the coastal defence duties.

In November 1916 the 1st Cyclist Division was broken up. The 2nd Royal North Devons amalgamated with the 2nd Royal 1st Devons to form the 4th (Royal 1st Devon and North Devon) Yeomanry Cyclist Regiment, still with 2 Cyclist Brigade. This brigade was based in Norfolk in the winter of 1916, but then moved to Ireland and was stationed at Longford until the end of the war.

The New Army in Devon
By the end of 1916 a man of military age had a number of options. He could sign up as a regular soldier for an army career. He could enlist into a service battalion for the duration of the war or volunteer

for the Territorial Force, perhaps for home service only. Or he could simply wait to be called up.

Those who volunteered to join the army tended to look towards the local regiments, but there were many exceptions. For example, the Royal Fusiliers (City of London Regiment) raised no less than seventy-six battalions during the war and its 23rd and 24th (Service) Battalions were better known as the Sportsmen Battalions. Rather than recruit from a small geographical area, these battalions were largely made up of men who had made their name in sports such as cricket, boxing and football. Serving with the 24th Royal Fusiliers was Private Arthur Alexander Stokes of Bovey Tracey. Some of Arthur Stokes' letters survive and in them he signs off as 'Art'.

Art Stokes was the son of James and Mary Stokes and was listed as a lawyer's clerk in the 1911 Census, but there are no clues to his particular sporting prowess. His father and youngest sister, Marjorie, stood at the gate of their house on Marlborough Terrace, Bovey, as Art swung his kit bag over his shoulder, waved goodbye and walked off to the railway station. That turned out to be the last time they saw him.

His last letter to his sister Marj was written only twelve days before he was killed and the address he gives is suitably

Private Art Stokes 24th (Sportsmen) Battalion, The Royal Fusiliers. (Roger Mitchell – Stokes family)

anonymous to steer clear of the censor's ink. It reads: A Section, Machine Gun Company, 5th Brigade.

Art's battalion (24th Royal Fusiliers) was in France as part of 5 Brigade, his 'address' referring to a machine gun company is particularly interesting. In 1914 the British Army went to war with each infantry battalion containing a machine-gun section with two Vickers machine guns. Experience showed, however, that to be fully effective machine guns needed to be deployed in greater numbers and crewed by specially trained men. To achieve this the Machine Gun Corps was formed in October 1915, but it took time to train men and deploy them effectively. It is entirely plausible that 5 Brigade may have pooled their battalion machine guns to form a machine gun company, of about twenty Vickers guns, as Art's letter seems to suggest.

In this letter to his sisters Art Stokes wrote that he was 'pretty well and manage to pull along all right, of course, with a lot of grumbling etc. – that's only natural for a Tommy. I hope though that the war will be over before the winter, as I shouldn't like another one out here.' He also wrote that he was pleased to get Marj's letter and added that he 'was in the trenches at the time but am not at present. The village our company is billeted in only boasts one small shop, but never mind I don't suppose we shall remain here long.' The rest of the letter consists of cheerful and kindly teasing comments to his two little sisters and ends, 'I am your affectionate brother, Art xxxx.'

Whatever his sport, Arthur Alexander 'Art' Stokes was killed in action near Thiepval village on the Somme battlefield on 30 July 1916. He was 22 years old.

Enlistment

The picture of volunteers enlisting over the page shows the crowd which assembled to see off volunteers from Salcombe from outside Great Western Railway office, Fore Street. The high spirits surrounding this event are encapsulated in the bus notices which read, 'Excursion to Berlin' and 'Berlin only'. The volunteers are,

Volunteers enlist for the front, Salcombe 1914. (Cookworthy Museum, Kingsbridge)

from left to right: P. Yeoman, N. Spry, R. Martins, J. Gillard, M. Oare, G. Wood, I. Cooper, R. Heath, W. Distin, Dare, T. Clements, A. Cook and L. Skentlebery.

The 8th Devons was the first service battalion formed by the Devonshire Regiment in the Great War. The regiment was raised in August 1914 from a nucleus of officers and NCOs from the 1st Battalion and was permitted to call itself General Buller's Own, after Sir Redvers Buller VC of Crediton.

It was quickly followed by a second service battalion, the 9th Devons, with which it would serve very closely until 1918. Their junior officers were initially recruited from the universities, the public schools and from the Artists' Rifles. Not all who volunteered did so to bear arms. The Reverend F.L. Hines, resident Wesleyan minister in Kingsbridge, became an army chaplain on 23 June 1915.

Many men old enough to enlist did so. Others had to wait a while; 7 January 1915 was Martin John Damerell's sixteenth birthday. Like numerous other boys his age, he decided it was time to 'do his bit'. Living in Curtis Knowle at the time, he travelled down to Kingsbridge to enlist.

Martin John Damerell, always known as John, was the son of Martin George and Elizabeth Damerell. He was born in Diptford, but the family moved to a small house in the village of Woodlands, now a part of Ivybridge. He was one of eleven children, a large family, some of whom still live in the town. John worked at Stowford Mill, in the paper making area. Mill records first show his name in May 1913 and he appears for the last time January 1915, suggesting that he joined the army in February or March 1915. He enlisted into the Devonshire Regiment and was posted to the 9th Battalion.

John Damerell of Woodlands, Ivybridge in the uniform of a private of the Devonshire Regiment (John Stacey – Damerell family)

John Damerell was not alone. Robert Anstiss, the son of Robert Anstiss of Highland Street, Ivybridge, was also serving in the 9th Battalion. Brothers Sydney and Rupert Downing of Cadleigh Park joined up together.

Training

The 10th Devons were raised in September 1914. Their training began soon after, as units of 79 Brigade, including the 10th Devons, began to assemble in the Salisbury Plain area from September 1914.

Khaki uniform and equipment were not generally available until later in 1915 and in the meantime everything was improvised. There was also a degree of improvisation in organisation as the following incident shows.

Cyrus Greenslade, who went on to serve as a brigadier general in the Second World War, was aged 22 in 1914. Like many others, he was a member of the Officer Training Corps at school and had been invited to attend an OTC training camp when war broke out. There it emerged he had been promoted to lance corporal. On the basis of this very slender military experience, Greenslade was

The band of the 10th Devons training in 1914. (Author's collection).

granted commissions in no less than three battalions of the Devonshire Regiment, the 4th, 5th and 10th. He went to see the commanding officers of both the 4th and 5th Devons only to find their offers were into 2nd line battalions (i.e. for home service only) so off he went on his motorbike to Codford where the 10th Devons were based. There he met:

> '*one of the real characters of the Devonshire Regiment, Colonel (George) Ellicombe who wore the ribbons of the Kandahar Star, the Tirah…and three of South Africa. He was raising the battalion with the help of some Militia and Special Reserve officers. The remainder were from the Inns of Court, Artists Rifles or, like myself, from school.* [Greenslade explained his dilemma and Ellicombe said] . . . "*well here you are and here you will jolly well stay – the battalion is arriving at the station in an hour's time – you will go and meet it and bring it here.*"'

Greenslade didn't argue. He met about 1,000 men at the station, most of them in civilian clothes. In the picture below the 10th Battalion is marching in line and its soldiers look to be properly uniformed. This suggests the picture was taken after mid-November and probably in the Bath area, as Aggett states that it was not until then that the soldiers' kits were complete. The battalion trained alongside the other battalions in 79 Brigade (the 8th Duke of Cornwall's Light Infantry, 12th Hampshires and 7th Wiltshires).

Training centred upon marching and drilling; musketry and trench digging. The role of experienced NCOs in this training was vital, and in 1914 almost all the sergeants in the 10th Devons came from the Old Comrades Association. The 10th Battalion seems to have been unusually well provided in this respect, as at this time the Divisional Commander ordered that officers and NCOs take their drill books on parade with them. By the time it left Bath in April 1915, the soldiers of the 10th Devons were capable of marching 100 miles in a week whilst carrying full packs – and as Lieutenant Greenslade noted *all dismounted officers carried exactly the same kit and equipment as the men'*.

The 10th Battalion, The Devonshire Regiment in training. The Commanding Officer, Colonel George 'Jelly' Ellicombe, is riding in the front. Behind him are two other officers, the one on the left is Major Emerson. (Author's collection)

Rugby Team, 10th Battalion, the King's Own Royal Lancaster Regiment at Kingsbridge, summer 1915. (King's Own Royal Regiment Museum, Lancaster)

Sport was an essential part of the training as well as recreation provided for the men. Boxing, football and rugby were particularly popular.

Following a long period of training, in and around Aldershot, the 8th and 9th Battalions were posted to France in 1915. There they were to stay and take part in a number of important actions. The 10th Devons was also sent to France in September 1915, however, the battalion was not to remain on the Western Front. In November 1915 the 10th Devons moved to Salonika where it remained for the duration of the war.

July 1916 – the Somme Offensive

The Battle of the Somme has become one of the iconic actions of the Great War and it is here that the 8th and 9th Devons were put to the test.

The 9th Battalion was one of the few British units to reach its initial objectives on the first day of the battle. However, this achievement came at terrible cost. Of the 775 soldiers of the 9th

Devons who attacked at dawn on 1 July, 463 were dead, missing or wounded. Only one of the battalion's officers was unscathed.

William Noel Hodgson volunteered at the outbreak of the war. He wasn't from Devon – his father was the Bishop of Saint Edmundsbury and Ipswich. Hodgson fought at the battle of Loos in 1915 where he was mentioned in despatches and awarded the Military Cross. By all accounts, he was a very popular junior officer, well known to the men of the 8th Devons as well as his own battalion. He was the 9th Battalion's bombing officer on the first day of the Battle of the Somme.

Lieutenant William Noel Hodgson MC, 9th Battalion, Devonshire Regiment (unknown)

The 9th Devons' jump off point was a trench close to a small woodland called Mansell Copse, and their objective was the German-held village of Mametz. Captain Duncan Martin, the officer commanding A Company was worried by a German machine gun by the shrine in a civilian cemetery which overlooked the open ground – known as Shrine Alley – across which his men would have to attack .

Hodgson, an Oxford graduate, had been writing poetry since at least 1913 and started publishing poems in periodicals at the beginning of 1916. He is probably best remembered for the poem 'Before Action', which was published just two days before he died. It is a commonly held belief that the poem was written with the premonition of his death, from his knowledge of the German machine-gun positions that lay in front of the 9th Devons' objective on 1 July.

> ### Before Action
> *By all the glories of the day*
> *And the cool evening's benison*
> *By that last sunset touch that lay*
> *Upon the hills when day was done,*

By beauty lavishly outpoured
And blessings carelessly received,
By all the days that I have lived
Make me a soldier, Lord.

By all of all man's hopes and fears
And all the wonders poets sing,
The laughter of unclouded years,
And every sad and lovely thing;
By the romantic ages stored
With high endeavour that was his,
By all his mad catastrophes
Make me a man, O Lord.

I, that on my familiar hill,
Saw with uncomprehending eyes
A hundred of thy sunsets spill
Their fresh and sanguine sacrifice,
Ere the sun swings his noonday sword
Must say good-bye to all of this; -
By all delights that I shall miss
Help me to die, O Lord.

The 8th Devons formed part of the brigade reserve on 1 July. It was in action within three hours of the beginning of the attack and suffered 208 casualties. A and B companies were decimated by the same machine gun that had killed Martin, Hodgson and so many soldiers of the 9th Devons. About 3.30pm the last reserve company, C Company, 8th Devons was also ordered forward. The officer commanding C Company was Lieutenant Eric Savill. Having seen the carnage taking place to the east of Mansell Copse, Savill used his initiative and chose to take an alternative route. Using cover provided by a slight rise in the ground to the north-west of the trees, C Company achieved their objective – the Hidden Wood – with light casualties.

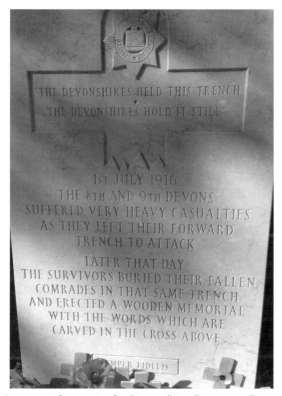

A memorial stone in the Devonshire Cemetery, France

At the end of the first day of the Battle of the Somme the bodies of many men of the 8th and 9th Devons were retrieved from where they had fallen. They were carried back to the front line trench position and buried in a section of it. On 4 July a ceremony was held at the burial site of the 161 soldiers from the Devonshire Regiment. A wooden cross was put up at the time by the survivors. Carved on the cross was the inscription: 'The Devonshires held this trench, the Devonshires hold it still'.

The graves were left in this position when the cemeteries were rebuilt after the war and there are now 163 graves in Devonshire Cemetery. The words of the original inscription are on a stone memorial at the cemetery entrance. The dead include Captain Duncan Lenox Martin and Lieutenant William Noel Hodgson.

Corporal Theo Veale with other NCOs of the Devonshire Regiment. Veale is wearing the Victoria Cross which he was awarded in 1916. (The Keep Military Museum, Dorchester)

Private Theodore William Henry Veale VC

Theodore Veale was born in Dartmouth on 11 November 1892. He enlisted into the 8th Battalion, the Devonshire Regiment. On 20 July 1916 east of High Wood on the Somme, Private Veale was out with stretcher parties when he heard news that C Company's commanding officer – Lieutenant Eric Humphrey Savill – was missing.

Veale went out and located Savill, who was wounded and lying in corn just 50 yards from the German trenches. He managed to drag the wounded officer into a shell hole, where he left him and went to fetch water. He returned with water and tried to drag the officer back, but couldn't move him. He went back to the British trench again, this time returning with a number of volunteers, corporals Allen and Lord. They put Savill on a groundsheet and managed to drag him 50 yards, when the Germans opened fire and Corporal Allen was killed. Veale and Lord left Lieutenant Savill in another shell hole.

At dusk, Veale went out yet again, this time with volunteers including Lieutenant Duff and Mr Crosse, the battalion chaplain. They located the injured Savill, but a German patrol opened fire on them. Duff held the Germans at bay with just his revolver whilst Veale crossed no man's land again, got to the British trenches and retuned with a Lewis Gun. Duff and Veale were now able to put down effective covering fire whilst the others got Lieutenant Savill safely back.

It may be difficult for those of us who have not served in the armed forces and for whom war is observed at a distance to understand actions such as those of Private Veale and Lieutenant Duff.

In trying to make sense of such acts of bravery, the fraternal and familial bonds formed between these men should not be underestimated. An army battalion is the home and family of the soldier, and strong bonds are formed between officers and men alike. Private Veal had enlisted into the 8th Devons and had known no other unit. He had trained with them and fought on the first day of the Battle of the Somme with them.

The truth is yet more complex. The wounded officer Veale rescued was not just any officer. It was the same Lieutenant Eric Savill who had saved the lives of many soldiers from C Company on 1 July by using initiative and avoiding that deadly German machine gun in Shrine Alley. It seems fitting, then, that the memorial gardens in Dartmouth are named the Veale-Savill gardens.

The war memorial in the Veale-Savill garden in Dartmouth. The garden also contains magnolias donated from those in the gardens at Royal Windsor. (Author's collection)

Mr Crosse the battalion chaplain was also visible on 1 July, always up in the front line with the stretcher-bearers, helping the wounded, and it was he who buried the fallen 8th and 9th Devons in the Devonshire Cemetery.

Theodore Veale VC (The Keep Military Museum, Dorchester)

Lieutenant Duff, who held off a German patrol with his pistol whilst Veale went back for the Lewis Gun, had proved himself cool and brave in action. On 1 July, he was ordered to find survivors from A and B Companies and take them further forwards in attack, which he did. After seeing off the German patrol and rescuing Savill, Duff was seen to climb a small tree near to battalion HQ and retrieve from it the medical officer's bandages. When asked what on earth he was doing, Duff explained that the white bandages were attracting enemy fire.

For his acts of gallantry Private Theodore Veale, 8th Devons, was awarded the Victoria Cross and later promoted to corporal. Lieutenant S.H. Duff and Lieutenant Eric Savill, 8th Devons, were each awarded the Military Cross; both were later promoted to captain.

After the war, Eric Savill went back to Cambridge, graduated in 1920 and joined his father's firm of chartered surveyors. He took the post of Deputy Surveyor at Windsor in 1930, managing an extensive and varied estate and was promoted to Deputy Ranger in 1937. He was knighted in 1955 and the Savill Gardens at Windsor have become his living memorial. Theodore Veale also survived the war. Both Savill and Veale died in 1980.

By 3 September 1916 the 8th and 9th Devons had been fighting continuously since July and were behind the lines resting when they were unexpectedly summoned back to the front, the message interrupting an officers' football match.

On 6 September the 9th Devons – only 400 strong by this point

The Vice-Chairman
Imperial War Graves Commission

Begs to forward as requested a Photograph, taken by
the Director - General of Graves Registration and
Enquiries, of the Grave of :—

Name *Damerell.*

Rank and Initials *Private. m. J.*

Regiment *Devons.*

Position of Grave *Delville Wood Cemetery.*

All communications respecting this Photograph should quote the
number (C35W/35//7/9) and be addressed to :—
IMPERIAL WAR GRAVES COMMISSION,
82, Baker Street,
London, W. 1.

Owing to the circumstances in which the photographic work is carried on, it is
regretted that in some cases only rough Photographs can be obtained.

[M1306) 36357/W213 12m 2/2b G & S E. 7297.

Official postcard received by the parents of Martin John Damerell following his death in 1916. (John Stacey – Damerell family)

– attacked alongside the Gordon Highlanders just east of Delville Wood near Ginchy. They suffered very heavy casualties. One of the survivors, Company Sergeant Major Randell, reported to HQ afterwards that the damage was done by enemy machine-gun fire and British shells falling short of their target. The regimental history states that eight officers and 100 men were killed, wounded or missing.

John Damerell died on 6 September 1916, aged just 17. He died alongside Corporal Robert John Anstiss, aged 25. They are both buried in the Delville Wood cemetery. The fact that they are buried so close to the battle suggests that they were killed in action.

News of their deaths reached home soon afterwards. John Damerell's family still has the postcard sent to them showing John's grave in Delville Wood Cemetery, France.

By 1918 the full complement of the Devonshire Regiment was:

1st Battalion, 2nd Battalion, 3rd (Reserve) Battalion, 1/4th (Territorial) Battalion, 2/4th (Territorial) Battalion, 3/4th (Cyclist Training) Battalion, 1/5th (Prince of Wales' Territorial) Battalion, 2/5th (Prince of Wales's Territorial) Battalion, 3/5th (Prince of Wales's Territorial Cyclist Training) Battalion, 1/6th (Territorial) Battalion, 2/6th (Territorial) Battalion, 3/6th (Territorial Cyclist Training) Battalion, 1/7th (Territorial Cyclist) Battalion, 2/7th (Territorial Cyclist) Battalion, 3/7th (Territorial Cyclist Training) Battalion, 8th (General Buller's Own Service) Battalion, 9th (Service) Battalion, 10th (Service) Battalion, 11th (Reserve) Battalion, 12th (Labour) Battalion, 13th (Works) Battalion, 14th (Labour) Battalion, 15th Battalion and the 16th (Royal 1st Devon & Royal North Devon Yeomanry) Battalion.

In May 1919 the Devonshire Regiment supplied a rifle company of volunteers to join the 1st Oxfordshire and Buckinghamshire Light Infantry. They were detailed to reinforce the Allied Expeditionary Force in North Russia.

Originally, Allied soldiers had been sent to Russia to prevent the Bolsheviks supplying ammunition and military equipment to the Germans. Following the 1918 Armistice the expedition carried on to help the anti-Communist coalition in the Russian Civil War. In a campaign that has been described as 'confused, fruitless, hazardous and uncomfortable', the Devons fought with honour. In the battle of Ust Vaga, on 1 September 1919, six decorations for gallantry were awarded.

The Devons were at last withdrawn at the end of 1919 as the Allied Expeditionary Force left Russia.

Ten battalions of the Devonshire Regiment fought overseas: in France and Belgium, Mesopotamia, Salonika, Macedonia, Egypt, Palestine, Italy and in North Russia. They lost more than 6,000 men killed and about three times that number wounded. Many came from Devon, but some did not. Between them they were awarded two Victoria Crosses and 1,265 other gallantry awards and mentions in despatches.

Local men in other regiments

With conscription came the end of regional and county ties to regiments. There were two reasons for this. First, the decimation of some service battalions because of the terrible casualties suffered during the Battle of the Somme, and the effect on civilian morale when news of these came home, brought about a deliberate attempt never to repeat the mistake of placing so many friends and relatives together in battle. Second, the effects of casualty attrition during the war brought about the need for numerous replacements; put bluntly conscripted men filled the gaps.

This policy of allocating conscripts to where they were most needed means that there is often no pattern to the postings of individuals. In many cases, however, this was true before conscription. Whilst the local regiments were an obvious choice, personal reasons affected requests for service in particular units. For example, Private Jake Horton, son of Jarvis and Rhoda of Ivybridge, was posted to the 10th Battalion, The Queen's Own Royal West Kent Regiment and died near Ypres in June 1917.

Some army units, often those requiring men with specific skills, advertised in local newspapers. For example, in February 1915 the Army Service Corps advertised in the *Kingsbridge and South Devon Gazette* for men used to working with horses, grooms, blacksmiths etc.

Others soldiers moved around, serving in different battalions of the same regiment according to need. For example, Coventry George Warrington Carew was the son of the vicar of Chelston, Torquay and he was a captain in the 7th Battalion, the Dorsetshire Regiment. However, when he was killed in November 1916 he was serving as a major in the 1st Dorsets. Sadly, Major Carew, a member of the Ashburton Freemason's Lodge, has no known grave and is commemorated on the Thiepval Memorial, Somme.

Some local men joined or were posted to army units of the Dominions, out of necessity or because they had moved abroad to live. Private William Mann of Ivybridge fought and died on the Somme in May 1917 with the 10th Battalion, the Australian Infantry Force. Sydney Churchward, born in Buckfastleigh in 1893 and one of twelve children, married and moved to Toronto, Canada with his wife, Sadie. Sydney was a police officer, but he enlisted in Toronto and was posted to the 3rd Battalion, Canadian Infantry (Central Ontario Region). His Attestation papers show that he enlisted and was passed fit on 20 September 1916, aged 24 years and five months. He was 5 feet 10 inches tall with 40 inches of girth, a fair complexion, red brown hair and hazel eyes. Sydney Churchward, a Presbyterian, was killed in action in November 1917 and is commemorated on the Ypres (Menin Gate) Memorial.

Whilst William Mann and Sydney Churchward fought with 'colonial' units, William Robert Hambly did more or less the opposite. Though born in Plympton, Hambly had North American parents; he was the son of Robert and Rhoda Hambly who came from Illinois, USA. William joined the 5th (Prince of Wales's Territorial) Battalion, the Devonshire Regiment and was killed in action on 30 September 1918, aged 22.

Militarised South Devon

William Kenny from Drogheda, County Louth, was a regular soldier having fought in the Boer Wars. He was a 34-year-old drummer in the 2nd Battalion, the Gordon Highlanders when war broke out. On 23 October 1914 near Ypres, Belgium, Drummer Kenny fearlessly saved machine guns on two occasions by carrying them out of action. On numerous other occasions he carried urgent messages under very dangerous circumstances over fire-swept ground. Were that not enough, Kenny then rescued five wounded men under very heavy fire. For these feats he was awarded the Victoria Cross and promoted to Drum Major.

What is Drummer Kenny's connection to South Devon? In 1915 he broke his wrist and was sent to Devon to recover at the VAD

Drummer Lance Corporal William Kenny, 2nd Battalion, the Gordon Highlanders, photographed at the VAD Hospital, Newton Hall. Kenny is flanked by Dr Keily, Roman Catholic Bishop of Plymouth, and a local priest, Father Barney. The chevrons on his upper arms indicate Drummer Kenny's rank; the inverted chevrons on his left arm are overseas service stripes. Note also the tartan trews of the Gordons. (Totnes Image Bank)

hospital, Newton Hall. Kenny attracted so much attention because his was the first VC to be awarded in the Great War. Drummer Kenny became a celebrity!

The Roman Catholic community of Newton arranged the presentation of a valuable antique set of mother-of-pearl rosary beads and a gold crucifix to Kenny, which was presented by the Bishop of Plymouth. The Reverend Father Barney read the brief description of Kenny's action. Drummer Kenny VC later travelled to London where he received a 12-gun salute and under the eye of the Lord Mayor of London and Aldermen, and he was presented with an inscribed gold watch given by the Worshipful Company of Musicians. On arriving home in Ireland he was presented the freedom of the town of Drogheda by the Mayor and Corporation. William Kenny died in England in1936.

Just as local men were joining up and leaving the county, men from other parts of the country were coming to Devon for a multitude of reasons – all connected to the war, and not all were tales of valour and success such as Drummer Kenny's. For example, in 1915 Private Joseph Clarke of the East Surrey Regiment was walking along the cliffs near Stoke Fleming when he fell and injured his head. The local bobby, PC Friend, with the aid of a 300-foot long rope, eventually reached him, but found him to be dead.

In the late summer of September 1915 a Black Watch officer was seen around Torquay. He was decorated with the Distinguished Service Order and had in his possession a letter confirming the award of the Victoria Cross for bravery. However, suspicion was aroused when the cheques he was cashing were discovered to be fake. He was arrested at Torquay and turned out to be a deserter from the Royal Army Medical Corps.

In December 1915 another deserter, Serrington Hodder, a soldier of the Royal Garrison Artillery, was arrested in the South Hams by PC Tozer. On his way to Kingsbridge, Hodder jumped out of the horse-drawn trap near Collapit and PC Tozer gave pursuit, eventually finding and re-arresting him.

The King's Own Royal Lancaster Regiment in South Devon
To further complicate the picture of mobilisation, recruiting and training of troops in South Devon, army units from other parts of the country were stationed and billeted in the area. One of these army units was the 10th Battalion, the King's Own Royal Lancaster

Group photo of soldiers of the King's Own Royal Lancaster Regiment, believed to have been taken in Kingsbridge 1914 or 1915. (Cookworthy Museum, Kingsbridge).

Regiment – King's Own for short. The 10th King's Own was based in Devon from the outbreak of war until the summer of 1915 and a special relationship of sorts seems to have developed between the people of South Devon and the battalion.

On 7 August 1914 the 3rd (Special Reserve) Battalion of the King's Own was mobilised and left Lancaster for its war station: Saltash, Cornwall. It consisted of all the recruits from the Lancaster Depot, and about 600 regular reservists. The King's Own recruited in Lancashire, but a new service battalion, the 10th, was formed at Saltash some time in August – or maybe as late as September – 1914. Lieutenant Colonel Joseph Bonomi was the commanding officer and his battalion soon moved to Kingsbridge.

By Christmas 1914 250 soldiers from the King's Own were billeted in Kingsbridge. What effect did the posting of so many men in and around Kingsbridge have on the local population? Though there were concerns at first, the 10th King's Own seem to have been popular in South Devon. Christmas went very well. Parties for the men were given in both the Wesleyan and Congregational Church schoolrooms in Kingsbridge, where roast beef dinners were served, followed by plum pudding. These were followed by music and singing – 'Tipperary' and 'Hold Your Hand Out (you naughty boy)' – and, according to the local paper, a stage performance by Private Hughes who turned out to be *'a first class comedian'*.

On Boxing Day there was a smoking concert in Kingsbridge Town Hall which reportedly went *'with a merry swing'* and in January 1915 the sergeants of the battalion gave a whist drive and dance for the town. On 5 April the King's Own gave a dance that went on until 2am the following morning!

In January Sergeant Major Instructor Chapman arrived in Kingsbridge to train the men of the 10th King's Own. Chapman was a boxer and held the Army and Navy heavyweight title. The training went well, but there were the occasional accidents. Sergeant James Hanson had been a regular soldier with the 2nd King's Own. He had previously retired then re-enlisted. Old soldiers such as he were vital to the efficient training of the New Army. In March 1915 Henson was concussed in an accident suffered whilst drilling the troops. Another unfortunate accident happened at the Kingsbridge Market Hall on Tuesday evening 16 March, when Drummer Pearson sustained severe head injuries whilst being tossed in a blanket. Pearson was unconscious and had to be taken to Kingsbridge Cottage Hospital but he made a good recovery.

Private Alfred George Stirling is a less than typical example of men from the King's Own, and he is the one and only soldier of the battalion based in South Devon to be mentioned by name; and for one very good reason. Alf Stirling deserted!

Born in West Ham, the son of Mr and Mrs M.A. Stirling of 297 Queen's Road, Upton Park, Alf had a pre-war job as shop assistant. He enlisted into the King's Own at East Ham on 18 August 1914 and was posted to the 10th Battalion; he was 19 years old. For reasons unknown, Alf Stirling deserted at Kingsbridge on 4 January 1915 and this was reported in the *Police Gazette* on 19 January. He was re-united with the army sometime later and eventually

A postcard dated 1916 showing soldiers – believed to be from the King's Own Royal Lancaster Regiment – boarding trains at Kingsbridge. It is possibly winter 1915 when these troops were bound for Sunderland. (Cookworthy Museum, Kingsbridge)

All that remains of the railway station at Kingsbridge. The shed with the distinctive windows can be seen. (Author's collection)

promoted. He was killed in action in Belgium on 9 October 1917 whilst serving as a lance corporal in the 1st Battalion, the King's Own. He is commemorated on the Tyne Cot memorial.

The 10th Battalion soon numbered 900, almost full strength. In February 1915 a crowd turned out at Kingsbridge Railway station when between 400 and 500 men were transferred to the 3rd Battalion which had meanwhile been moved to Sunderland.

The band of the 10th King's Own must have been a particular good one, for the local newspaper reported that it contained no less than nine members of the well-known Besses o' th' Barn brass band from Whitefield (now Greater Manchester). On Saturday, 17 April 1915 the 10th King's Own band gave one of their last concerts in Kingsbridge, for in May the battalion moved on for good.

At the same time as elements of the 3rd Battalion moved back to Plymouth, the 10th received orders to vacate their Kingsbridge billets. The battalion assembled outside Kingsbridge Town Hall at 11pm and at half past the order 'quick march' was given. The men marched to Kingsbridge station and boarded trains for Swanage which left at midnight. There was no cheering and it was a sad farewell to the much respected soldiers of the 10th King's Own.

There were, as may be expected, a number of minor problems. Once the battalion's departure became known about the local newspaper ran a piece advising those who might have 'claims' against the 10th King's Own how to proceed. Lieutenant Colonel Bonomi had published an open letter stating that Army Regulations did not permit him to make deductions from soldiers' wages to pay for any of their bills, and urging any resident of South Devon with a claim to take this up with individual soldiers before they left. On the whole, however, Bonomi, the quartermaster, Lieutenant Whitaker, and the NCOs of the 10th King's Own seem to have done a fine job in maintaining good relations between the battalion and residents.

The 10th Battalion, the King's Own never saw active service and it became the 43rd Training Reserve Battalion in 1916. However, many, if not most, of those officers and soldiers who had been based in Kingsbridge transferred to other units once their training had been completed.

Does the time in Devon help explain the interesting story of Sergeant William Dillon? Sergeant Dillon served with the 8th Battalion, King's Own. He was born in Bolton, enlisted in Manchester and was killed in action 26 September 1917. He has no known grave, but is commemorated on Tyne Cot Memorial to the missing, Zonnebeke, Belgium. Interestingly, Sergeant William Dillon is also commemorated on the war memorial in Modbury though his connection with Modbury is unknown. Perhaps he had been 'adopted' by a Modbury couple whose own son was serving overseas. Or does some romantic liaison explain this connection? We shall probably never know.

Some South Devon men joined the King's Own. For example, Private Alfred Joint of Ilsington, near Newton Abbot joined the 8th Battalion. He died on 5 October 1918, aged 24, and was buried in Ilsington (St Michael) Churchyard. He was the son of Edward and Elizabeth Joint of Widecombe-in-the-Moor.

Lieutenant Horace Heptonstall Backhouse MC, was a member of the Erme Freemasons' Lodge and son of George Backhouse the landlord of the New Inn, Ermington. He was commissioned (as a second lieutenant) into the 10th Battalion of the King's Own on 10 June 1915 – the battalion that had been on his doorstep for the previous eight or nine months. Was this a coincidence? Officers were drawn from all over, often from public schools and university Officer Training Corps. There was also local commissioning into the battalions. For example, the 5th King's Own moved to Didcot in August 1915 and there were Didcot men in the battalion. Clearly they were encouraged to join this 'foreign' battalion which had suddenly become local to them. The same may well have happened in Horace Backhouse's case. He may have come across officers of the 10th King's Own and was encouraged by them to join their regiment.

Lieutenant Backhouse was attached to one of the King's Own regular battalions in November 1916 and then the 7th Battalion from

April 1917. He was promoted to full lieutenant and awarded the Military Cross for leading a trench raid on 7 June, in which he was wounded. The citation in the *London Gazette* reads:

> *'For conspicuous gallantry and devotion to duty. During a daylight raid on enemy trenches he successfully led his platoon into the enemy second line, subsequently bringing back his whole company with one officer and sixty prisoners.'*

He was later mentioned in despatches for his work in another action. He was moved to the 8th Battalion in July 1918, but sadly was killed in action on 23 August 1918.

Home on leave

No doubt servicemen home on leave thought themselves safe – if only for a short while. Periods of rest and recuperation were vital to supporting the morale of the troops. Sadly, accidents meant that South Devon was not always the safest of places to be as the following two stories illustrate. Both tales involve soldiers of the 7th (Cyclist) Battalion, the Devonshire Regiment (Territorial Force), which was on coastal defence duties.

Stanley Dent and friends during army leave. Cars seem to have been a part of Stanley Dent's life. We don't know where the open top car came from, but after the war Stanley ran the Bantham Garage at Thurlestone. (Cookworthy Museum, Kingsbridge)

Private Stanley Southwood of the 7th Devons was only 17 when he and a friend decided to strip off and go for a swim at Bigbury-on-Sea. Private Southwood did not appreciate the strength of the tide between the coast and Burgh Island and he drowned. He was the son of Sam and Annie Southwood, of Bradninch (near Cullompton) and his grave is in St Lawrence churchyard, Bigbury.

In January 1915 two off duty British officers were caught up in a dramatic and tragic incident in Torquay. Flight Sub-Lieutenant Bertram Welby Hart, a pilot in the Royal Naval Air Service, was a former pupil of the Devonport High School for Boys, Plymouth. He was based at the Royal Naval Air Station, HMS *Pembroke*, but contracted pleurisy and was sent home to his parents' house on sick leave. On 24 January 1915 – the day after his 22nd birthday – he went for a drive to Torquay with his friend Lieutenant Ernest Simpson, of the Amy Service Corps and Mr Murton, a Marconi electrician from Plymouth.

As they drove into Torquay the off duty officers were halted on Belgrave Road by sentries of the 7th Devons – privates Botterill, Harris and Pullman.

In order to make sense out of what happened next, it is worth noting the following points. It was thought that an armed enemy (a German spy perhaps) was in the area. The soldiers of 7th Battalion on sentry duty had specific orders to watch out for any suspicious vehicles and/or persons. Their instructions were to search cars and if required to detain any passengers. These orders must be understood in context. Spy scares were not rare – especially prior to and at the beginning of the war. In 1911 Oberleutnant Max Shultz had been sentenced to twenty-one months in gaol for spying. After the outbreak of war there was a multitude of spy scares in Devon. For example, in September 1914 suspected spies were reported to police in Brixham, Plymouth and South Molton. In May 1915 three men were arrested in Okehampton on suspicion of spying and later that year (July) Scotland Yard issued an alert asking the public to be on the lookout for an escaped German PoW.

Both privates Harris (aged 19) and Pullman (aged 28) were very new to the army, having enlisted only the previous month.

Given the above factors, it is safe to assume the sentries were nervous if not frightened. It was dark and there were no NCOs in the immediate area. The off duty officers were no doubt irritated at being stopped and searched. As usual, the sentries were armed with loaded rifles.

The sentries searched the car and became suspicious because its registration number was chalked onto cardboard. Perhaps they assumed it was fake. They sent a runner to fetch their sergeant and demanded that the officers waited until he arrived. As they waited Private Pullman ordered them to move the car to the side of the road as a tram was approaching. This resulted in an altercation between the sentries and officers and there are a number of accounts of what happened next.

According the other sentry, Private Botterill, Lieutenant Hart became firm with them, pointing out that he was a British Naval officer, giving his service number and insisting that he had letters to prove that he was Sub-Lieutenant Hart. In response, Private Harris replied robustly something like: 'Shut up your yap! I don't want to see any letters. Stand there and wait 'till my colour sergeant comes.'

'Don't talk to me like that,' replied Hart. 'Do you know to whom you are talking? That you are talking to your superior officer.'

Throughout this argument the sentries held their rifles at the ready.

By now a crowd had gathered and somebody sent for the police. PC Mugridge was soon at the scene and in the midst of the argument he pushed into the crowd. A shot was fired. Lieutenant Hart was hit in the face and fell down dead. Lieutenant Simpson who was standing behind Hart was shot in the left armpit by the same bullet. He was taken to Torquay hospital where he later died.

Private Harris was consequently charged with causing their death. His colleague, Private Pullman, with aiding and abetting. Harris confessed that his rifle had been fired, but insisted it was an accident. After three days of trial, on 4 February the court decided that Lieutenant Hart and Lieutenant Simpson were killed by accidental fire by Private Harris during execution of his duty. It was recommended that the military should select more experienced men to be placed on highway duties.

Flight Sub-Lieutenant Bertram Welby Hart is buried in his family plot at Ford Park Cemetery, Plymouth and Lieutenant Simpson in a Commonwealth War Graves Commission grave in the same cemetery.

PART 3

The People's War

Hospitals, VAD and convalescent

The Red Cross in Devon had started work on plans to create hospitals and convalescent homes by 1909, these were to help relieve pressure on the military hospitals in the case of war. Generally these were known as Voluntary Aid Detachments (VADs). By the start of the war, Devon had sixty Detachments with a county personnel of 1,500 men and women. The hospitals were generally well equipped with furniture, medical equipment and cooking appliances.

With its VAD system, The Red Cross was able to provide temporary and convalescent homes with staff at short notice. Detailed plans were in place for mobilisation. In May 1914 a test mobilisation on a large scale was held and temporary hospitals were prepared and equipped.

When first established in 1909, there was little understanding of how such a voluntary group could organise into an effective adjunct to the military hospital system. There were no handbooks or instruction manuals available and little or no assistance from the authorities. Devon VAD, like the other county branches, had to work out for itself a systematic approach.

In administrative terms there was a county structure within which areas close to the parliamentary constituencies were semi-autonomous. A system akin to triage was put into operation in the

Nurses at the Collapit Creek VAD Hospital, Kingsbridge. The group of nurses are named Balkwill, Hyde, Yeabsley, Quarm, Blumtag, Loman and Coyte. (Cookworthy Museum, Kingsbridge)

establishment of the hospitals themselves. In the area covered by this book First Line hospitals were established at Torquay (370 beds) and Newton Abbot (150 beds). Second Line VAD hospitals were set up at Buckfastleigh (50 beds, officers only), Dawlish (15 beds), Ivybridge (50), Kingsbridge (24), Paignton (50), Salcombe (40), Totnes (75) and Yealmpton (16). The patients at these VAD Second Line hospitals were generally less seriously wounded than at other hospitals.

In addition to the above large numbers of public and private buildings (often large houses) were turned over for use as small hospitals, most of which operated as annexes to nearby larger hospitals. For example, Mr George Chaloner, a bank manager from Totnes, offered his property, Strathmore, which occupied a secluded position off Bridgetown Hill, Totnes, as a VAD hospital for wounded soldiers. Local women working under Dr Chapman and

Miss Tregaskis, who took up duties as matron, prepared Strathmore for the casualties.

At Christmas 1915 the *Totnes Times* reported:

> *An ample supply of Christmas Fare reached the VAD hospital at Strathmore. The wards were bright and decorated with flags, evergreens and seasonal mottoes. The King's message was received with pleasure. There were individual gifts for each of the 21 wounded soldiers. A concert in the evening was enjoyed by all and at dinner time Dr Chapman carved and was assisted by Miss Tregaskis (matron) and Nurse Moisey.*

Follaton House was placed at the disposal of the Devon Red Cross by Mr and Mrs Carey and it soon became a Voluntary Aid Hospital, remaining open for the duration of the war. Only convalescing soldiers – other ranks – were housed in the house itself, and they were known as 'the boys in blue' due to the blue uniforms they wore. Convalescent officers were billeted at the Seven Stars Hotel

The VAD hospital at Follaton House, Totnes. (Totnes Image Bank)

Follaton House, headquarters of the South Hams District Council in 2015. (Author's collection)

in Totnes. When visiting, their families lodged with people in the town. When the Armistice was declared an impromptu concert was organised at the hospital and the mayor and friends were invited.

Convalescent hospitals did not have the usual civilian meaning of convalescence. From March 1915 onward they were there to keep recovering soldiers under military control. For example the new residence convalescent home at Sharpitor, on the slope of Bolt Head, Salcombe, was opened by Mrs Mildmay. The property was loaned to the Red Cross Society by the owners, Mr and Mrs George Vereker. They wanted to provide accommodation for a convalescent home in memory of their youngest son Second Lieutenant Robert Humphry Medlicott Vereker, 2nd Battalion, the Grenadier Guards, who was killed in action at Landrecies on 25 August 1914, aged 27.

At the official opening Captain Craig announced Sharpitor would be classified as a Second Line Voluntary Aid Hospital with twenty-five beds and adapted as a convalescent home with electric light and a billiard room. Due to its distance from town, Sharpitor also had staff accommodation.

Mrs Turnville Foster was the matron, Miss Warren was commandant and Miss Montgomery, quartermaster. Dr Twining organised the staff of eighteen Red Cross nurses. At the time of opening eighteen soldiers were expected during May and soon after the full complement of twenty-five. In the summer of 1915, wounded soldiers from Sharpitor were treated to tea at Hope Cove, though the planned tea on the beach was not possible due to the poor weather. Nevertheless, the men no doubt appreciated the treat as girl guides in uniform served them tea and afterwards sang for them.

Some hospitals were developed as, or soon became, specialist units. Categories of specialism included mental hospitals, units for limbless men, orthopaedic units, cardiac units and typhoid units. For example, the Seale Hayne Neurological Hospital, Newton Abbot, was a specialist neurological section for other ranks, and

Mrs F.B. Mildmay opens the Sharpitor for Soldiers, May 1915. (Totnes Image bank)

Eggbuckland Hospital, Plymouth was a specialist venereal disease hospital for thirty officers and 180 men.

The VAD aimed at training volunteers to the same standard as probationer nurses. A rule of thumb was that they should be able to assist in the care of serious cases under the supervision of doctors or professional nurses. However, whilst the training system coped before August 1914, with the rapid expansion of casualties and the associated growth in the number of volunteers, many volunteers with little training were posted to hospitals.

The crime writer Agatha Christie, who was born in South Devon, joined the VAD in 1914 and attended wounded soldiers in Torquay, where a VAD hospital was established in the Town Hall. Christie first served as a volunteer nurse, but in early 1917 she qualified as a 'dispenser' and as such earned the princely sum of £16 a year until the end of the war.

In an interview given to the Imperial War Museum when she was 84 years old Christie recounted her experiences in Torquay hospital during the war. She describes writing letters to the girlfriends of wounded servicemen, walking with the men when they went for X-rays, feeling ill whilst watching a stomach operation and cleaning up after amputations. She also records her sadness at the death of one soldier she cared for.

It was as a dispenser that she learnt much about poisons, and this came in handy in her later career as a crime writer. She began her first novel, *The Mysterious Affair at Styles*, in 1916. The plot unfolds with the detective, Hercule Poirot, as a Belgian refugee, and with Captain Hastings convalescing from the war. In the plot money for the war effort is being raised.

Like Christie, most VAD volunteers were of the middle and upper classes. Being unaccustomed to hardship and traditional hospital discipline, the VADs were at first an uneasy addition to any military hospital's rank and order. They lacked the advanced skill and discipline of the professional trained nurses and were often critical of the nursing profession. Relations improved, however, as the war went on. The VADs generally increased their skills and so the professional nurses became more accepting of their contribution.

Clerks and cooks were trained and, in addition to the VADs, in many cases, women from the neighbourhood also volunteered on a part time basis.

As well as the military and VAD hospitals a number of civilian hospitals were used for the treatment of servicemen. These included Torbay Hospital (75 military beds), Torquay Western Hospital (115 beds), Brixham Cottage Hospital (10), Dartmouth Cottage Hospital (15), Newton Abbott Infirmary (44) and Teignmouth Civil Hospital (20).

Private hospitals, often for officers only, were established through the generosity of the comfortably well off. These included the Barrington Officers' Hospital in Paignton; Everest Officers' Hospital, Teignmouth; Flete, Ermington; Froyle House Officers' Hospital, Torquay; Mazonet Officers' Hospital, Stoke Gabriel; the Honourable Mrs Burns's Hospital for Officers, Stoodley Knowle and Torquay and Manor House Officers' Hospital, also in Torquay. Private convalescent homes were also set up across the county, for example, the Cleeve House, near Ivybridge. In Paignton and Chudleigh there were hospitals established solely for the treatment of wounded Belgians.

The 4th Southern General Hospital in Plymouth catered for 193 officers and 1,029 other ranks and included a specialist neurological section for other ranks. This hospital needed a second line hospital especially for the treatment of 'Neurasthenic' patients and Stowford Lodge in Ivybridge was ideally located for such use. These Neurasthenics were men suffering a condition of the nervous system that would nowadays be termed a mental illness – the symptoms were fatigue, anxiety, headache, heart palpitations, high blood pressure, neuralgia and a generally depressed mood.

Stowford Mill produced fine quality paper well into the present century. The Lodge, had at times been the owners' house, then manager's and up until February 1917 it was used by the Devonshire School of Gardening. However, in 1917 the Lodge was lent by the owners of Stowford Mill – John Allen and Sons – for the duration

A photograph taken outside Stowford Lodge Second Line Hospital, Ivybridge. The men in the photograph ware a variety of dress. Some are hatless, others ware forage caps and, in one case, the tam o'shanter of a Scottish regiment. Some are dressed in civilian clothes and others in Hospital Blues. (unknown)

of the war and Miss Deare of Blachford gave permission for fallen trees to be used as firewood and allowed fishing in the River Erme.

In December 1917 Stowford Lodge opened as a second line VAD Hospital with fifty beds and continued in this capacity until January 1919. The assistant commandant of the hospital was Mrs Alice Hawker of Chantry, mother of Captain Reggie Hawker (who had died of wounds in Egypt in a month earlier), whilst the assistant quartermaster was Mrs Clapperton, the mill manager's wife.

The 4th Southern General Hospital provided a matron and a number of trained nurses under the supervision of an officer of the Royal Army Medical Corps, but the domestic management and some nursing duties were undertaken by VADs. The hospital was equipped and liberally supported by the residents of Ivybridge and the surrounding area, with help from the Totnes Divisional VA Hospital Funds.

However, in 1918 the War Office took exception to the deployment of military nurses in a VAD unit and so the professional staff along with the Neurasthenic patients were moved and the hospital was reorganised with complete VAD staff for normal convalescing patients. During its period of operation, the Stowford Mill hospital admitted a total of 267 patients, including 154 suffering from neurasthenia.

In general, the servicemen tended to prefer the voluntary and private hospitals to military ones. They were not so strict, were less crowded and the surroundings more homely. For example, the Kingsbridge VA Hospital was housed at Collapit Creek House, lent rent free by Lieutenant Commander Froude, Royal Navy Volunteer Reserve, and his wife. Collapit was a very nicely situated country house with extensive grounds and we can only imagine how it seemed to men injured by the ravages of a horrible war.

Collapit was established as a VA hospital in January 1916 and carried out its work until July 1918. At first there were just twenty-four beds, though this was increased to twenty-nine in May 1918. In all, a total of 460 patients were admitted to the hospital. From May to July 1918, five beds at the Kingsbridge Cottage Hospital were put to use as an annex to the VA hospital itself. The hospital was supported by subscriptions and donations from Kingsbridge, South Brent and the surrounding neighbourhood. The staff at Collapit came mostly from the South Brent area, though some probationer nurses were recruited in Kingsbridge.

There was a standard uniform for hospitalised and convalescent servicemen which consisted of a blue single-breasted jacket with a white lining, blue trousers and a white shirt with a red tie. The lapels were originally designed to be fastened at the neck, and so when turned back showed the portion of white lining. Neither the jacket nor matching trousers had pockets. To complete the outfit servicemen wore the service cap or hat of their own unit, with its

Patients at the Collapit Creek VAD Hospital, Kingsbridge. The men are named Turner, Hirn, Francis, Brenton, Rafferty, Richards, Catt, Leigh and Adams. The Hospital Blues can clearly be seen in the photograph. (Cookworthy Museum, Kingsbridge)

regimental badge. The suit was also known as the Blue Invalid Uniform, the Hospital Suit and Hospital Blues.

The Blues tended to be ill-fitting as they were manufactured in few sizes. Many servicemen had to turn up cuffs and trouser bottoms to fit. When washed, the outer fabric shrank at a different rate to the lining, resulting in yet further problems.

There were many complaints about the poor quality and bad fit of the hospital clothing. Eventually questions about the inferiority of these uniforms were raised in the Houses of Parliament, but to no avail and the military authorities required that Hospital Blues be worn at all times by soldiers. Officers, however, were exempt and instead were provided with a white armband bearing a red king's crown.

The military hospital at Seale Hayne near Newton Abbot holds a special place in the history of the Great War in South Devon. This was where Major Arthur Hurst, Royal Army Medical Corps, carried out much of his pioneering work on shell-shock patients. Hurst took the men to the peace and quiet of the rolling Devon countryside where they could work on the farm and where they were encouraged to use their creative energies interspersed with intensive therapy sessions. The treatment was a form of what nowadays could be termed 'occupational therapy' and was revolutionary in its time.

Funded by the Medical Research Committee, Hurst filmed shell-shocked patients home from the war in France. Using Pathé cameramen, Hurst's films concentrated on soldiers who suffered from intractable movement disorders as they underwent treatment at the Royal Victoria Hospital, Netley (near Southampton) and undertook programmes of occupational therapy at Seale Hayne. His are some of the earliest UK medical films and which were initially used to illustrate Hurst's lectures.

Great claims were made at the time, not least by Hurst himself, of 'miracle treatments' that enabled him to cure ninety per cent of shell-shocked soldiers in just one session. It has been suggested more recently, however, that Hurst was alert to the wider appeal of the motion picture and saw in it an opportunity to position himself favourably in the post-war medical hierarchy. It is also suggested that some of the before treatment shots were re-enacted specifically for the camera. Claims made of 'cures' in the film and associated publications by Hurst were challenged by other doctors treating shell-shock. The absence of follow-up data and evidence from war pension files suggested that Hurst may have overstated the effectiveness of his methods.

The American Women's War Relief Hospital was established at Oldway Mansion, Paignton, in September 1914. The mansion was originally built by Isaac Singer, the sewing machine magnate. After his death it was converted by his son, Paris, to resemble the Palace

Oldway mansion in 2015. (Author's collection)

of Versailles; the gallery on the first floor is a reproduction of the Hall of Mirrors at Versailles.

In the Great War Oldway was again converted. Randolph Churchill urged Paris Singer to offer up his residence and it was converted into a 600 bed, perfectly equipped hospital. Oldway's reception rooms were adapted to make wards to accommodate 250 beds and the rotunda to house rows of beds for wounded soldiers. In all over 2,000 patients were admitted. Singer also provided £5,000 toward the equipment and so Oldway was equipped with an up to date operating theatre.

The hospital unit consisted entirely of surgical and medical staff from the USA, Dr Beal being appointed Chief Surgeon. On 3 November 1914 Queen Mary visited Oldway Mansion bringing a present of 300 pieces of clothing and visited each ward, expressing her delight in the care and efficiency she saw.

Stretcher-bearer C.H. Bond remembers the hard work carrying wounded men up and down stairs from any of the 230 beds to various other departments. It was conducted in the most agreeable conditions, however, as the building is noted for its grand staircase made from marble with balusters of bronze. The ceiling over the staircase is decorated with an ornate painting based on an original design for the Palace of Versailles by the French painter and architect Joseph Lebrun.

Following his affair with the dancer Isadora Duncan and, it has been suggested, in order to avoid UK tax, Paris Singer became a United States citizen in 1917. He eventually emigrated to the USA and Oldway mansion was no longer the permanent home of the Singer family. It became the Torbay Country Club in 1929. Paignton Urban District Council purchased Oldway Mansion from the Singer family in 1946 and until 2013 the building was used as council offices. In January 2007 Torbay Council announced that it was considering selling the mansion as it had become too expensive to maintain. Plans for Oldway Mansion to be converted into a luxury hotel and sheltered retirement flats were approved and a deal struck with property developers. Sadly, since October 2013, Oldway

Lady Paget Ward visits the American Women's War Relief Hospital at Oldway, Paignton, 1914. (Totnes Image Bank)

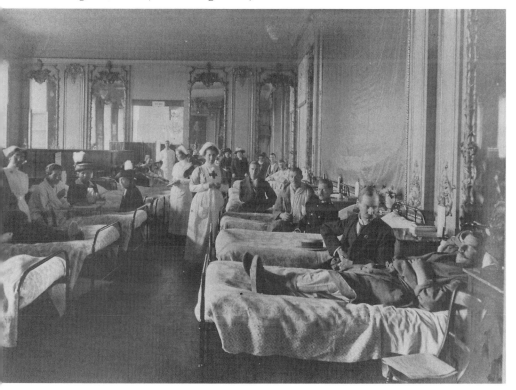

The rotunda at Oldway Mansion in 2015. (Author's collection)

Mansion has been empty and the building is becoming increasingly run down.

Prisoners of War

In the autumn of 1914 2000 people turned up at the Torquay Pavilion to attend a meeting on 'Enemy Aliens in Our Midst' at which Lord Clifford and Lord Leith pointed out the danger to security posed by Germans living in South Devon and advocating the internment of all of them. It was somewhat ironic then that at the height of the 1918 harvest 600 Germans PoWs were working on Devon farms. The arithmetic was simple. Agriculture could not cope without manpower and there were many PoWs in Britain: 150,000 by the end of 1917.

The first German prisoners of war were received at Dorchester Camp – a hastily converted army camp – in August 1914. This camp became permanent and was used throughout the war. Suggestions that Austrian and German PoWs might be put to work on farms were made early on in the war, but initially met with local opposition.

Attitudes changed and by 1917 there was extensive use of German prisoners for work outside the PoW camps. Under the Hague Convention it was permissible to put PoWs to work, though officers were exempt. The work was not to be excessive or connected with the operation of the war.

By 1918 all German prisoners, barring the officers and the physically unfit, were working. Prisoners were paid for their work at the same rate as British soldiers. The work was varied and included labour in quarries, building work, putting up huts, road repairs, land reclamation, etc. By the autumn of 1918 70,000 prisoners were working, 30,000 on the harvest, under the direction of local Agricultural Committees.

German prisoners of war working at Denbury. The soldier on the left is thought to be Johann Grandyl who lived at Higher Wotton. The plough is a very early version of a 'Butterfly' or 2-way plough, which was designed to turn over at end of furrow to ensure all soil turned same way. (Totnes Image Bank)

German prisoners of war who were billeted in the Kingsbridge workhouse. (Cookworthy Museum, Kingsbridge)

In South Devon there were eleven PoW depots by 1918, each with 35-50 prisoners under the armed guard of men from the Royal Defence Corps. In Kingsbridge the German PoWs were housed in the old workhouse. Of the farms around Ashburton there were forty-two where Germans were working and another forty-two around Newton Abbot. Prisoners received 25s a week pay, with 15s deducted by the army for board and lodging. There are no reported attempts at absconding and it is easy to see why. Faced with the choice between a war spent in honest hard work on a farm or a risky escape that would lead back to the trenches, most PoWs were content to stay in South Devon.

Perhaps unsurprisingly, nationally only four German PoWs escaped during the war. Two are believed to have died in the North Sea and two reached Germany. Gunther Pluschow published an account of his escape in 1922 called *My Escape from Donnington Hall.*

Keeping so many German prisoners was an expensive business. Some men of the 7th Devons were put on guard duties. For example, Private George Harvey was guarding prisoners at the Holyport PoW camp near Maidenhead. George, born in Buckland Tout-Saints (near Kingsbridge) was an old ex-regular, having served in South Africa with the 2nd Devons. He rejoined during the war. Sadly, George took ill whilst on duty and died in Maidenhead hospital.

Volunteering to 'do our bit'

'Totnes Ladies Working Party: 45 prs socks, 34 scarves, 9 prs mittens and 30 mosquito nets. 10,000 cigarettes from Mrs Mabel Collins have been received since the start of the war
Totnes Times, 4 March 1916

Mr H. Jarvis of Fore Street, Kingsbridge collected money to buy eight packets of Woodbine cigarettes to be sent to India for the 'Kingsbridge lads' serving there with the 5th Devons. Some weeks later, in July 1915, Lieutenant W. B. Beer, 5th Devons, wrote to him thanking him for the gift which the men greatly appreciated.

From the onset of war there were numerous individual and group efforts. Men too young, too old, or deemed unfit to fight, or in a reserved occupation, might join the National Guard or the Volunteer Training Corps, both of which were well represented in the area.

Funds were set up to help the war effort, or to provide aid for those suffering from the war's effects. Some were national, such as the War Savings schemes, the Red Cross and the Belgian Refugee Fund.

Guns, sometimes captured ones, were taken around towns all over the country to persuade people to invest in War Bonds and War Savings Certificates. In November 1918, just as news of the Armistice came through, the result of Gun Week War Savings in South Brent amounted to £2,742 15s.

Local funds included the Devon Patriotic Fund and the *Western Morning News* War Fund. Support came not only from subscriptions

Kingsbridge Cadet Corps in 'war savings' parade, 1918. (Cookworthy Museum, Kingsbridge)

November 1918 – South Brent Gun Week. (Totnes Image Bank)

and donations, but from specially organised events: concerts, dances, outings, shows, teas, whist drives and so on. In late August 1914 an open-air concert was held at Tor Cross for the *Western Morning News* War Fund and 160 people attended.

In April 1915 a Girls' Club had started meeting in the Ivybridge Church Hall on Monday nights. As well as dancing and being entertained by occasional singers, the ladies there were busily knitting mufflers, socks, mittens and cuffs to be sent to soldiers and sailors. There was a similar group of women in Totnes making 'comforters' – mufflers, Balaclavas and mittens – for the troops. Such support was so popular that in 1914 Weldon's of The Strand, London, released through the local newspapers a picture pattern for knitted sleeping 'Balaclava' style helmets.

Women all over the area of South Devon made sandbags. In September 1915 a working party in Kingsbridge sent 300 sandbags to the front. Others collected eggs or vegetables for the wounded, with the local press regularly carrying news of their most recent efforts.

The war increased demand for both cotton and wool. Wool was used extensively in military uniform – Cold Harbour Mill near Cullompton produced woollen puttees for the army throughout the war. Cotton was needed – amongst many other things – for uniforms, bedding sheets and dressings.

Each soldier carried a wound dressing which could be used on himself or on a comrade. There were also shell dressings for larger wounds and paraffin gauze dressings. The scale of casualties increased dramatically and it was estimated that a wounded soldier needed on average twenty dressing changes. It was soon estimated 50 million dressings per year would be needed by the army. Cotton dressings became expensive and in short supply.

Sphagnum moss had been used since ancient times as a dressing as it was found to have both absorbent and antiseptic properties. Two ounces of dry

TOTNES

Aeroplane Week

begins next

MONDAY

IF, during the week beginning next Monday, the subscriptions from Totnes and district for National War Bonds and War Savings Certificates reach the total of £20,000, the authorities will give to an Aeroplane the name of our town.

Think of our civic pride if we read in an official despatch that

the Aeroplane "TOTNES"

has carried the war into German territory and harried the lines of communication of the foe—perhaps that it has saved Totnes men from the deadly attack of the Hun, enabling them to return unharmed to their wives and children.

Do your duty during Totnes Aeroplane Week

Have your Money ready for Monday—ready to buy National War Bonds and War Savings Certificates — ready to help in making Totnes Aeroplane Week a triumphant, a record success.

Get your Pass Book. See how much money you have in the Bank. Draw the cheque and have it ready to give Totnes's effort a flying start, on Monday morning.

Totnes Aeroplane Week. (Totnes Image Bank)

moss could absorb two pounds of liquid. The antiseptic was later identified as iodine, naturally occurring in the moss. Sphagnum moss grows in waterlogged conditions. From 1915 onwards, it was collected in Canada, Ireland and Scotland and from the mires and bogs of Dartmoor. It was approved as a dressing in 1916 by the War Office.

Collection on the moor might be done by hand or using a rake. Then the moss was squeezed hand-dry and sent for processing. There was a moss processing centre in Princetown which was funded by the Prince of Wales. Totnes and Dartmouth were also processing centres. Princetown became the headquarters and depot for processing, with women dressed in white overalls working in whitewashed rooms. First the moss had to be carefully picked over, removing any foreign bodies such as small twigs of bracken or heather. Then it was washed in a solution of 'corrosive sublimate', mangled to squeeze out excess liquid, then dried by hot air from a furnace for three hours.

The moss was then distributed to local centres where dressings were made, many of which sprang up in the small towns and villages on the edge of the moor. There were some very specific instructions about how the dressings were to be made. To fill the dressings, loose moss that was already well picked over and quite dry was to be filled into the muslin bags until each bag weighed one ounce (for large dressings). For medium dressing, three-quarters of an ounce of moss was used, and half an ounce for the small dressings. The filled bags were to make a firm but elastic pad in which the moss was uniformly distributed. To close the bag, the open end was to be folded twice upon itself and sealed with a running thread. The dressings were then shipped off to the military, but only sterilised once they reached the hospitals.

In the Dartmoor village of Widecombe there is a 15-inch shell which serves to commemorate the contribution of the village's children to the war, as they were the local collectors of the Sphagnum moss from the moor. Mrs Bates, the headmistress of Widecombe in the Moor Council School, organised the children to go onto the moor to collect moss. The first large sack of moss was sent to the Exeter VAD by Mr H. Hannaford JP, a school governor.

A group of local women processed and dispatched Sphagnum moss wound dressings from a workshop in Totnes. They were organised by Mrs Kate Chaloner, wife of a Totnes banker, and Mrs Mary Maye the wife of Thomas Maye, a cider producer from Staverton. The volume of dressings produced by these women was enormous. Over 27,000 dressings made from Dartmoor moss were sent to Exeter in two years. All were made by volunteers in shop premises at 44 Fore Street which had been donated by Mr Hayman.

The women travelled to Dartmoor to collect the moss, using trains from Totnes station to Buckfastleigh or South Brent. They had to raise the money to finance the operation themselves, and this was done by holding fetes, social events and even a competition to guess the weight of the town's mayor. Kate Chaloner was very keen on arranging musical evenings as she played the piano and accompanied singers at these events.

PART 4

War in the Air and at Sea

View from the clouds

On 15 September 1916 Flight Lieutenant E.F. Monk took off from Pembroke piloting the airship SS.42. The SS (Submarine Scout or Sea Scout) class airships were small non-rigid airships, developed as a matter of urgency to counter the German U-boat threat to British shipping. A total of 158 were built, each armed with bombs and a Lewis Gun.

SS.42 was scrambled to search for a German submarine which had been reported near Lundy Island in the Bristol Channel. The poor weather that day forced Monk to return after a couple of hours, nothing sinister having been sighted. However, a gust of very strong wind caught the airship as Monk attempted to land and it slammed into the ground. Ropes broke loose, the port suspension ripped off and the wireless operator was thrown out. Then SS.42 soared upwards with fuel pouring out of the ruptured tanks, reaching a height of around 7,000 feet. Further damage resulted and she rose another 1,500 feet, but somehow Monk managed to cling on.

Now SS.42 was blown in a southerly direction by the air current. The airship covered around 100 miles over the next three hours before beginning to descend. Slowly at first, but then faster, the airship spiralled down to earth. Flight Lieutenant Monk was able to

Ground crew manoeuvring a Sopwith biplane at East Prawle RNAS base (East Prawle History Society)

A.J. Edlin poses with one of the biplanes based at East Prawle (East Prawle History Society)

jump clear just before the SS.42 hit the ground, injuring himself but escaping anything serious. When help arrived, Monk enquired about his whereabouts and discovered that he was on Dartmoor close to the village of Ivybridge.

The wreckage of the SS.42 was recovered and rebuilt as SS.42a. The following year she was again damaged and drifted out to sea, killing both crew members.

There was a Royal Naval Air Service station at East Prawle during the war. After 1916 it was equipped with Sopwith 1½ Strutters, a multi-role biplane used by the RNAS for coastal patrols. The hangars at East Prawle were made of canvas and resembled very large tents. Local man – A.J. Edlin, formerly a butcher – served as an engineer at the base.

Flight Lieutenant J.S. Mills became a local celebrity in 1915 after bombing a German Zeppelin base in Belgium. He was the son of John Edward Mills, owner of Mills Brothers' Old Brewery, Wolborough Street, Newton Abbot and a tied estate of six public houses. Mills joined the Royal Naval Air Service soon after the outbreak of war, having never flown before. He had, however, made a large model aeroplane in his father's yard, but it never got off the ground. Mills was interviewed by the local press, who reported that he was *'a keen cricketer, a capital bowler'*.

This story has a sad ending, however. Brewer Mills had two other sons in the armed forces. Cecil Mills served in the Army Service Corps and Edgar Mills with the 7th Battalion, the South Wales Borderers. Edgar, a lieutenant in 1915, was promoted to captain, but was killed in Salonika shortly before the war ended, aged 27. He won the Military Cross and was mentioned in despatches, but this may have been little comfort to his family.

Home waters

The war raged in Start Bay, at times dangerously close to the Devon shore and so it is no surprise to learn that local men and local vessels were involved. As early as March 1915 the local press were reporting that a German submarine had been sunk in Start Bay, fouled by navy patrol boats.

The *Kingswear Castle* was a paddle steamer built in 1904 and working on the River Dart. A local rumour – much favoured nowadays by the operators of tourist boats on the Dart – is that she was used as a fever isolation hospital for soldiers of the Great War. When she was released back to her owners they were so fearful that contagion had infected her timbers that they stripped her of her engines, set her by the river bank and set fire to her rather than put her back into service.

Others have suggested a quite different story, however. Richard Clammer, writing on the Dartmouth Museum website, claims that the *Kingswear Castle*, though converted as an isolation vessel, was never actually used as such. This was because of an oversight by the Dartmouth Port Sanitary Authority who had not noticed that the legislation requiring them to have such a facility had lapsed some years previously. It was a costly mistake, for the boat was purchased and converted at great cost. Following resignations and reprisals, the boat was finally beached at Fleet Mill just below Totnes, presumably the cost of re-converting her proving too expensive.

What is agreed as fact, however, is that the steam engines of the original boat were re-used on another paddle steamer, also called *Kingswear Castle*. This one was built by Philip and Sons of Dartmouth in 1924 for the Great Western Railway Company, and she is still working. After providing summer excursions on the River Medway and the Thames for many years, the current *Kingswear Castle* returned to Devon in 2012 and began running excursions again on the Dart.

HMS *Formidable* was sunk in Start Bay on New Year's Day 1915. She was the second British battleship to be sunk by enemy action during the war and the first to be sunk in a submarine attack. The story of her sinking, however, also involves the brave crew of a South Devon fishing boat.

Formidable was a pre-Dreadnought battleship, laid down at Portsmouth in 1898, but only commissioned for service in 1904.

She was armed with forty 12-inch guns, forty-five 8-inch guns and had improved armour plating developed, ironically, by the German arms manufacturer, Krupp.

At the outbreak of war, HMS *Formidable* was based at Portland as part of the 5th Battle Squadron and assigned to the Channel Fleet to defend the English Channel. After covering the safe transportation of the British Expeditionary Force to France in August 1914, she took part in the transportation of the Portsmouth Marine Battalion to Ostend on 25 August. On 14 November, HMS *Formidable* and the other ships of the 5th Battle Squadron were moved to Sheerness because of fears that a German invasion was possible, even likely. The squadron was transferred to Portland on 30 December 1914, and *Formidable* began patrolling the Start Bay area of sea off the Devon and Dorset coast. The battleship spent the daylight hours of New Year's Eve participating in gunnery exercises off Portland, supported by the light cruisers HMS *Topaze* and HMS *Diamond*. After the exercises the ships remained at sea on patrol. German submarine activity had been reported in the area, but it was assumed that the rough sea conditions and the increasing wind would render submarine attacks too difficult to carry out. This assumption proved devastatingly wrong.

At just after 2am on 1 January 1915 a torpedo from a German submarine struck the number one boiler on the port side of the ship. At first, Captain Loxley thought the ship might reach land and be saved, but the vessel was taking on water quickly and began listing severely to starboard. About 2.40am the captain gave the order to abandon ship. There was no panic. The boom boats were launched, but darkness and worsening weather made it difficult to get the men and boats over the side. Some boats landed on the water upside down; even a piano was thrown overboard to be used as a life raft.

Whilst all the preparations to save the crew were being enacted, another torpedo struck the ship, about 3am. This one exploded on the starboard side, which was already partially submerged. There was wreckage everywhere. HMS *Formidable* was doomed and by now all the boats that could be launched were in the water. Survivors reported seeing the second in command, the ship's chaplain and Captain Loxley smoking pipes as the ship went down.

HMS *Topaze* and HMS *Diamond* came alongside and managed to pick up eighty men from open boats. It was reported that the men were scantily dressed – testament to the rapidity of events after the first torpedo struck – and that the small boats were half full of water. Other sailors were now swimming, clinging to wreckage or – if they were very lucky – adrift on a gale-blasted sea in a small, open boat with no provisions, no life belts and many oars unusable. One boat braved the raging seas and managed to reach Lyme Regis. There were fifty-one sailors aboard, forty-eight of whom survived. It had taken these men twenty-two hours to row approximately 40 miles from where *Formidable* had sunk to Lyme Regis; probably the fierce exercise of the rowing kept the men warm and stopped them falling asleep. The sailors were cared for in the Pilot Boat Hotel. They included Master at Arms Cooper and Knight, the ship's cook. It is reported that the landlady's dog, a rough-haired collie called Lassie, licked one seaman back to life. Six sailors from HMS *Formidable* are buried in Lyme Regis town cemetery.

Meanwhile, the fishing smack *Provident* was out that night in the fearful sea. *Provident* was a Brixham trawler (number BM291) built in Devon by Sanders and Company at Galmpton Creek on the River Dart. She was owned and skippered by William Pillar of Brixham, who had aboard a crew of two men, an apprentice and a cabin boy. *Provident*, like most Brixham smacks, had no engine. She was a gaff-rigged ketch, with two masts and three dark tan sails. In that gale she would have been well reefed, but even so the skipper, fearing she was becoming overpowered and unsteerable, ordered the crew to heave-to. This would slow the boat's progress and enable them to ride out the heavy weather.

Once hove-to, something was spotted in the sea. It was difficult to work out what this something was; so great was the swell that it would appear on the surface, then quickly disappear. It turned out to be one of HMS *Formidable*'s boats, with seventy-one sailors aboard. On sighting the fishing smack, the sailors had raised an oar with a shirt or jacket tied to it as a makeshift distress signal. It took five attempts and over three hours to transfer the sailors from their open boat onto the *Provident*, but eventually they succeeded – some of the men jumping over wild sea to the smack. The survivors were taken to Brixham. There is a memorial plaque to the crew of the *Provident* in Brixham and the events of New Year's Day 1915 are remembered in the town's museum.

Daniel Ferguson (also known as Daniel Taylor, after his stepfather) was the apprentice fisherman on board *Provident* that night. He played his part in the rescue, aged just 16. *Provident* herself was sunk by the German navy in November 1916, off Portland Bill. Daniel survived and later he joined the Royal Naval Reserve Trawler Section with whom he served from 1917 to 1919. Altogether, 547 men and the captain's dog – an Airedale terrier called Bruce – were lost when HMS *Formidable* went down; but 199 sailors survived. The body of the captain's dog Bruce was washed up near Abbotsbury, Dorset, and is buried there. In 1981 the wreck of HMS *Formidable* was found on the sea bed.

In April 1917 the destroyer HMS *Broke* rammed the German torpedo boat *G42* in the Dover Strait. The crews of both vessels were caught in hand to hand fighting. One of HMS *Broke*'s crew, Stoker 1st Class Frederick Carder, was killed and his body taken home to Paignton for burial. When HMS *Broke* broke free the German vessel sank.

On 4 February 1915 the commander of the German High Seas Fleet, Admiral Hugo von Pohl, sent out a general warning to shipping in the Imperial German Gazette. This warning made clear that the waters around Great Britain and Ireland, including the whole of the English Channel, were considered to be a war zone. From 18 February any enemy merchant vessel encountered in this zone would be destroyed, without warning if necessary.

On 20 March 1917 His Majesty's Hospital Ship *Asturias* – showing all lights and painted with a red cross for all to see – was attacked by a German submarine eight miles off the South Devon coast.

The hospital ship Asturias, *wrecked off Bolt Head. (Cookworthy Museum, Kingsbridge)*

HMHS *Asturias* was built in 1907 for the Royal Mail Steam Packet Company. She served for some years on the Southampton to Buenos Aires run. When war broke out the ship was requisitioned by the Admiralty and converted into a hospital ship. She had accommodation for 896 patients, but on one occasion due to very heavy casualties, she transported 2,400 sick and wounded.

Within a few months HMHS *Asturias* was put to work making regular crossings to France carrying back the wounded from the Western Front. She served in the Eastern Mediterranean during the Dardanelles Campaign, 1915, returning wounded from Gallipoli, Egypt and Salonika to hospitals in Britain.

On the night of 20 March, the *Asturias* was struck by a torpedo which made a large hole in her stern. She didn't sink, but drifted towards Bolt Head, where she wrecked on the coast. Fortunately, HMHS *Asturias* had previously landed her cargo of wounded at Avonmouth, but around forty members of the crew were killed and others wounded. Some of the survivors were towed in lifeboats into Salcombe harbour whilst the bodies of those killed were landed in Plymouth and Torquay.

After the torpedo attack the ship was written off as a total loss, but her hulk was put to use as a floating ammunition store at Plymouth for the rest of the war. After the war, the ship's hulk was repurchased by Royal Mail Line and rebuilt as a cruise liner, renamed *Arcadian* she operated Mediterranean and West Indies cruises until 1930; she was finally scrapped in 1933.

German attacks on shipping continued. On 28 April 1917 the P&O liner *Medina* was torpedoed by the *U-31* off Start Point. *Medina* had set sail from Australia with a mixed load of passengers and cargo which included meat and butter. There were six casualties.

In the Navy

'8th April, 1915. We left Alexandria today with Australian troops and horses on board, consisting of two well-equipped batteries, some men of the Army Service Corps, and a few infantrymen, forming part of the invading force of the Peninsula of Gallipoli.'

So wrote Wireless Officer David Curd, of Plymouth. He was one of the thousands who fought as sailors during the Great War. David's daughter, who lives in South Brent, provided extracts from her father's diary and personal letters.

Before the war, David Curd had worked for Marconi as a wireless engineer and he was drafted into the navy for his specialist skills in radio communication. In 1915 he was involved in the Gallipoli Campaign, and later in the war twice torpedoed by German submarines. He survived, and went on to play his part in the Second World War working in propaganda broadcasting.

Curd's Great War diary continues:

'25th April. It is now dawn and I am on watch. At about 0445 I hear heavy gun fire and on going out on deck discover that there is land in sight and about ten to fifteen warships as well as transports all around . . . there is a Russian cruiser and a French battleship tearing along at 20 knots in the direction

of Kim Kale... and with good glasses I can see our battleships, including the Queen Elizabeth, *roaring away with their large guns... The transport (ship)* River Clyde *is heading for the shore and has now beached herself. Gangways are dropped for her troops, the Munster and Dublin Fusiliers, to disembark via lighters...and as the men are rushing down the gangways the Turks have got the range and a veritable hail of bullets falls upon them; scores are killed, and the wounded falling into the water drag their comrades with them.'*

An examination of the war service of the sailors listed on the Ivybridge War Memorial sheds much light on the nature of service in the Royal Navy in 1914 – 1918. The first fact of note is that most of them spent their war below decks.

Albert Henry Prout enlisted in December 1915 and was a trimmer aboard His Majesty's Trawler *St Ives*. As a trimmer – or coal trimmer – he would work below decks, involved in all coal handling tasks. These began with the loading of coal into the ship. Once underway, Albert would have worked inside the coal bunkers located on top of and between the boilers. It was very hot work. The inside of a coal bunker was poorly lit, full of coal dust and extremely hot due to residual heat from the boilers. He would have used a shovel and wheelbarrow to move coal around the bunkers. It was essential to keep the load of coal level, or trimmed, because if too much coal built up on one side of a coal bunker, the ship would list to that side. Finally, Albert would shovel the coal down the coal chute to the firemen and stokers below.

Like the other trimmers, Albert would also be involved in putting out any fires in the coal bunkers. Fires occurred frequently due to spontaneous combustion of the coal and had to be extinguished with fire hoses and by removing the burning coal by feeding it into the furnace. Perhaps because of the small size of the trawler, Albert Prout doubled as the ship's cook. He died on board the *St Ives* in December 1916, killed when a mine exploded off Falmouth.

Then there were the stokers. Stoker (or fireman) is the job title for those whose job it was to tend the fire for the running of the ship's steam engine. The Royal Navy used the rank structure: ordinary stoker, stoker, leading stoker, petty officer stoker and chief stoker.

Richard John Blight and Thomas Carne were both petty officer stokers. Blight died on HMS *Vanguard* which exploded in July 1917, Carne on HMS *Garland*. James Henry Nichols, a leading stoker aboard HMS *Indefatigable* and Cecil Victor Screech (HMS *Defence*), were both killed during the Battle of Jutland in 1916, trapped and drowned in the bowels of their ships.

Stoker Francis Tozer was killed aboard HMS *Highflyer* in December 1917 when the French munitions ship the *Mont Blanc* exploded off Halifax, Nova Scotia. Charles De Ville was leading stoker on HMS *Exmouth*.

Albert Henry (Ted) Cole also worked below deck. He was an engine room artificer aboard HMS *Recruit*. Engine room artificers were fitters, turners or boilermakers competent in the working of engines and boilers HMS *Recruit* was torpedoed in 1917.

Of those eleven Ivybridge sailors, only four worked above decks. Arthur Pearce was shipwright 1st class on HMS *Hampshire* which sank in June 1916 with Lord Kitchener also on board. Yeoman of Signals George Hattrick (a signals petty officer) served aboard HMS *Thunderer*. He died more than a year after the Armistice on 2 December 1919 and is buried in the Ivybridge cemetery, leaving a widow, Annie.

Edwin Penwill and J. Symons, were both concerned with ship discipline. Penwill was petty officer regulating on HMS *Talbot*, Symons was a ship's master at arms (a ship's senior rating, normally carrying the rank of chief petty officer or warrant officer and in charge of discipline aboard ship).

There were many ways in which sailors may have been killed. The fates of two Ivybridge sailors, Francis Tozer and Charlie De Ville, and William Thompson of Ugborough illustrate some of the possibilities.

On 6 December 1917 HMS *Highflyer* – with stoker Francis Tozer aboard – on escort duties across the Atlantic, was anchored in the outer harbour of Halifax, Nova Scotia. Out of the inner harbour came a Norwegian ship the SS *Imo* travelling fast as she was behind schedule. At the same time the French munitions ship the SS *Mont Blanc* was steaming into Halifax. She was cruising up from New York, her hold full of explosives (gun cotton, picric aid and trinitrotoluene) and with barrels of highly volatile benzol loaded on her decks.

The two ships collided in The Narrows. The *Mont Blanc* did not explode straight away. She caught fire and Captain Le Medec ordered the ship to be abandoned. She drifted towards Halifax until she came to rest on a pier. At this point, a boat full of volunteers from *Highflyer* rowed out to see if they could help.

At about nine o'clock the *Mont Blanc* exploded. Sixteen hundred people were killed and an area of two square kilometres of Halifax destroyed. The explosion is reported to have been the largest in the war and it was such that the bodies of eight of *Highflyer*'s crew were splattered against the ship's superstructure.

Charlie De Ville was the son of John and Hannah De Ville who lived at 3 Western Road, Ivybridge. He joined the navy and by 1915 when he was aged 36, was a leading stoker on board HMS *Exmouth*, a Duncan Class battleship, launched at Birkenhead in 1901. She joined the 6th Battle Squadron in the Home Fleet on the outbreak of the war. The *Exmouth* was armed with four 12-inch guns in turrets, twelve 6-inch guns, twelve 3-inch guns, six 3pdr guns, two Maxim guns and four torpedo tubes. She had a top speed of 19 knots and a complement of 750 men. In February 1915 HMS *Exmouth* was docked at Chatham, Kent. Charlie De Ville and some shipmates went ashore on leave. On returning to the ship on 16 February Charlie fell into the water and drowned. He is buried in Gillingham (Woodlands) cemetery, Kent.

The generic rank of 'stoker' was also applied to any sailor who worked running the ship's engines. William Piper Thompson of Ugborough held the rank of stoker 1st class aboard the submarine HMS *J6*. The *J6* was a diesel-electric powered submarine which suffered an unusual and costly encounter off the Northumberland coast on 15 October 1915.

About 4pm the *J6* was on the surface off Blyth when she was spotted by the lookouts aboard HMQS *Cymric*. The *Cymric* was one of the Q-ships – heavily armed merchant ships with concealed weaponry. Q-ships were designed specifically to try to lure German U-boats into making surface attacks, thus giving the Q-ships the chance to open fire and sink them.

Unfortunately, the crew of the *Cymric* took HMS *J6* for a German submarine, perhaps mistaking the 'J6' painted on her conning tower for 'U6'. *Cymric* opened fire. A signaller was sent up to run up a recognition flag, but he was killed by shell fire. The *J6* then tried to lose *Cymric* by running into a fog bank. *Cymric* followed, sighted the sub sinking and took on survivors. It was only then that the mistake was noticed. Fourteen of HMS *J6*'s crew were killed including William Piper Thompson, aged 21.

A serviceman didn't need to be below decks to be killed when a ship went down. In fact, he didn't need to be a sailor at all. Sergeant Hall of the Royal Marine Light Infantry and a former resident of Ivybridge, died when HMS *Goliath* was sunk. HMS *Goliath* was commissioned in 1900 and served in the Far East until 1905, at which time she joined the Mediterranean Fleet. From March 1915 she took part in the Dardanelles Campaign in support of the landings at Gallipoli in April. *Goliath* was damaged by Turkish gun fire on 28 April and again on 2 May. On the night of 12-13 May she, along with HMS *Cornwallis*, was sent to Morto Bay off Cape Helles in support of French troops on the right-hand side of the Allied line.

The Turkish destroyer *Muavertet-i-Milet*, which at the time was crewed jointly by Germans and Turks, fired three torpedoes at HMS *Goliath* before escaping to safety. The first torpedo hit the *Goliath* by her forward 12-inch gun turret and she then began to list to port. The second torpedo hit the forward funnel. The ship continued to turn over and was nearly on her beam end when the third torpedo hit near her aft 12-inch turret. She then turned turtle, floated upside down for a couple of minutes and then sank bows first. Of HMS

Goliath's 700 strong crew, 570 died including her commanding officer, Captain Thomas Lawrie Shelford (aged 45) the son of Thomas Shelford, a successful businessman in Singapore who was a Companion of the Order of St Michael and St George. Captain Shelford left a widow, Mrs D. Shelford, of Swilly Lodge, Devonport. Also killed were Chief Petty Officer John Bunker, husband of Ellen Bunker, Modbury, and Marine Sergeant Hall.

Some servicemen were taken ill and died whilst on active service. If they were sailors, they may have been buried at sea. For example, Chief Stoker Fred Joint, husband of Emma Jane Joint, Blackawton, contracted pneumonia and died aboard HMS *Cornwall* on 30 March 1915. He was buried at sea. Fred Joint was aged 40, the son of Henry and Elizabeth Joint, South Brent.

Unlike the stokers and other below deck ranks, Lieutenant Commander Nigel Barttelot was probably on the Bridge of HMS *Liberty* when he was mortally wounded during the battle of Heligoland Bight in 1914. This engagement was the first pitched battle on the high seas. The British Navy had devised a plan to ambush German destroyers during their regular patrols. It was carried out by a British fleet of thirty-one destroyers and two cruisers, supported by submarines, six light cruisers and five battleships. The German fleet lost three light cruisers and one destroyer sunk, and three more light cruisers damaged. A total of 1,178 German sailors were killed or injured and 336 were taken prisoner. The British suffered one light cruiser and three destroyers damaged, thirty-five killed and forty wounded. Launched in 1913, HMS *Liberty* was a Laforey class destroyer, one of those damaged in the battle. Lieutenant Commander Barttelot was the son of Mrs St Aubyn of Halwell House, South Pool. He is buried in Stopham St Mary churchyard, Sussex.

Then there were the near misses. The Reverend G.H. Collier from Babbacombe was chaplain aboard the light cruiser HMS *Cressey* when she was patrolling in the North Sea off Ostend in September 1914. *Cressey* was torpedoed by a German submarine and sank. Collier survived by clinging onto a piece of flotsam for over two hours; 560 of *Cressey*'s crew died.

PART 5

Epilogue

The Fabric of South Devon

Reminders of the war are to be found all around Teignbridge, Torbay and the South Hams and an interested visitor could spend a happy couple of days touring and viewing them. Many of the sites of the 1914 – 1918 photographs in this book can be easily found.

Many of the VAD hospitals and convalescent homes are still standing and some can be visited. For example, at the time of

A procession in Kingsbridge to mark the 1935 Jubilee. The carnival float is called 'Hell Fire Corner – Great War dug out' and shows that the war was still in the foreground of popular imagination twenty years later. (Cookworthy Museum, Kingsbridge)

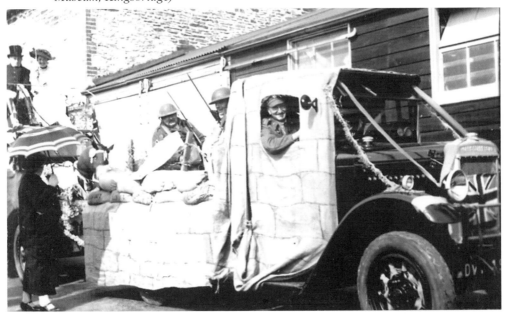

writing Oldway Mansion, Paignton, is empty but it is possible to stroll around the grounds. Sharpitor House, Salcombe, is now owned by the National Trust and houses the Overbeck's Museum, named after the scientist, Otto Overbeck – a prominent advocate of electrotherapy in the early twentieth century – who lived there between 1928 and 1937. Follaton House, Totnes is now the home of South Hams District Council and public access is permitted. The Seale Hayne site where Major Arthur Hurst pioneered his shell shock treatments is now a café and arts centre.

The second line Stowford Lodge hospital, Ivybridge can be rented as a holiday home. Restored and now known as Stowford Manor, it is complete with the beautiful stained glass window over the main staircase which shows Queen Elizabeth I crowning local MP and Vice-Admiral of her fleet, Francis Drake, in 1581.

It is even possible to live in a former Great War convalescent home near Ermington. The house and stables of the Mildmay's Flete House have been restored and refurbished and now comprise

The Ashburton Company, 5th (Prince of Wales's Territorial) Battalion, the Devonshire Regiment, 31 August 1918. The company is formed up outside St Lawrence Chapel, Ashburton, and seems to be about to march to Ashburton railway station which was further along the road from the chapel. The company includes Jack Yolland, George French, T. Gill. The civilian in shirtsleeves on the right is believed to be Jim French, blacksmith. (Totnes Image Bank)

View outside St Lawrence Chapel, Ashburton in 2015. (Author's collection)

twenty-nine exclusive self-contained serviced apartments described by a local estate agent as 'designed for an easy going lifestyle and relaxed environment, ideal as a main or a second home'.

Journeys from Totnes to Buckfastleigh, and Paignton to Kingswear can be taken by steam hauled trains as these two lines are now heritage railways run by volunteer groups. At Kingswear, a ferry still runs to Dartmouth where the former station building is now a café. A drive from South Brent to Kingsbridge provides glimpses of former railway buildings such as the former stations at Diptford and Kingsbridge and the tunnel entrance just north of Kingsbridge.

War memorials eventually sprang up in almost every town and village. Some are Lutyenesque obelisks, others more modest. They are to found on village greens, in churchyards and some inside the churches themselves. For example, in 1920 the vicar of St Petroc's, South Brent, announced that the war memorial committee had

Signal box and footbridge at Buckfastleigh railway station, now part of a heritage line. (Author's collection)

The entrance to the old railway bridge which took the Old Plymouth Road over the Primrose line north of Kingsbridge. (Author's collection)

collected £100 and they intended to erect a marble memorial inside the church. The names of the fallen were to be inscribed on it. In Totnes there was much discussion regarding the type of memorial, which names should go onto it and how to pay. Eventually, Mrs Chaloner and Mrs Maye, who had invested some of the funds raised for their wound dressing enterprise, made a substantial donation to the building of the Totnes memorial.

As well as the official memorials there are others in school halls, on railway platforms and elsewhere. Then there are the family memorials, usually in or around churches and usually only put there by the wealthiest families. This means that some servicemen have multiple commemorations of their sacrifice. For example, Lieutenant Robert Orlebar, son of a retired lieutenant colonel of the Royal Marines, has the following memorials: his gravestone in France; his name engraved inside the chapel at the Royal Military Academy, Sandhurst; on the Ivybridge war memorial and on the Roll of Honour inside St John's Church, Ivybridge. Also in St John's is the Orlebar family's memorial to Robert, unveiled in late 1915.

These memorials are continually in states of flux. For example, in November 2014 another soldier's name was added to the Torquay war memorial. Corporal James Radmore, 2nd Devons, was killed in France on 24 April 1918, aged 27. He has no known grave and until recently his name was missing from the Torquay war memorial. Research by the Royal British Legion proved that Corporal Radmore was from Torquay and so, deserved recognition on the memorial. This research inspired Torbay Council to honour him and add his name, and a representative of the Radmore family witnessed the unveiling of the plaque.

An element of romantic mystery still surrounds Corporal Radmore, however, as the only mention of him in the local press at the time was a brief 'killed in action' notice which simply recorded that he was the 'dearly loved sweetheart of Kate'.

A row of houses built in South Brent in 1914 was named Mons Terrace as a commemoration, perhaps a celebration, of that early battle. Number 44 Fore Street, Totnes, the former Red Cross

Captured German Field gun outside Totnes Castle. (Totnes Image Bank)

Dressing Depot where the Sphagnum moss was sorted, cleaned and packed, is still there – now housing a ladies hairdressing salon.

Lieutenant Colonel Windeatt Commanding Officer of the 5th (Prince of Wales's) Battalion, Devonshire Regiment asked the Mayor of Totnes to accept on behalf of the borough, the gift of a German field gun. The gun was captured by men of the 1/5th Devons during the last great advance. He thought it appropriate that one of the guns captured should find a resting place in the borough and suggested a tablet should be placed on the gun so that people should not pass it in ignorance of the circumstances under which it found a home in Totnes.

A number of servicemen died in the UK and are buried close to where they lived. For example, Major John Bayly of the Devonshire Regiment and Royal North Devon Hussars is buried in the family grave at Sheepstor, having died on 26 February 1918.

Those who take a boat trip on the River Dart may well see the hulk of the old *Kingswear Castle*. It is still on the Dart – now a rotten and barely recognisable hulk – but visible opposite Sharpham Point if one looks carefully.

South Devon, the Great War and literature

There are reminders in literature too. Henry Williamson's best known work must be *Tarka the Otter* which won the Hawthornden Prize for literature in 1928. He also created *Salar the Salmon*. Williamson joined the Territorial Army in 1914 and served with the London Rifle Brigade (5th Battalion, the London Regiment) and experienced the Christmas truce in 1914. After a gas attack in 1915, Williamson was invalided home and writing was encouraged as part of his convalescence. He recovered and went back to the trenches, and was later commissioned into the Machine Gun Corps.

Williamson's writing was profoundly influenced by the war he witnessed. He went on to write books and numerous articles about the Great War. Notable amongst these are *The Wet Flanders Plain* and *The Patriot's Progress*. One of Williamson's less well-known books is *On Foot in Devon*, published in 1933. The story goes that Williamson was approached by the publisher, Alexander MacLehose, in the summer of 1932 to write the Devon volume for his 'On Foot' travel series. Williamson agreed on the condition that he would write, not a straightforward travel guide, but a quirky, light-hearted yet serious mock guide. The research for this book

The Cloth Hall in ruins.

Marlborough church from the north. (Author's collection)

brought Williamson to the coast of South Devon. He rented a cottage in the South Hams and it is reported that shivers went along Williamson's spine every time he caught sight of Marlborough Church, it reminded him so much of the Cloth Hall at Ypres.

Rupert Sherriff was commissioned as a captain in the 9th East Surrey Regiment in which he served from 1915 to 1918. He fought at Vimy and Loos, and was awarded the Military Cross. He was badly wounded at Passchendaele in 1917. After the war he continued his writing and wrote his seventh play, *Journey's End*, in 1928. This play was firmly based on Sheriff's experiences of war. It was given a single Sunday performance in December 1928 at the Apollo Theatre, with the 21-year-old Laurence Olivier in the lead role.

It later ran for two years at the Savoy and is still popular today. The play was also performed at Dartington Hall, Totnes, and soon after the New Inn in Ringmore, near Challaborough, changed its name to *The Journey's End*.

Although Sherriff also wrote a number of successful film scripts – including *Goodbye, Mr Chips* (1939) and *The Dam Busters* (1955) – *Journey's End* is regarded as his masterpiece and is evoked by the eponymous pub in Ringmore. Whether or not there is any substantive link between Sheriff, the play and the pub is largely irrelevant for a trip to Ringmore is almost essential for any residents or visitors to South Devon who are interested in the Great War. The war memorial – which is a stained glass window best viewed from inside All Hallows Church — must be one of the finest in the county, if not the country.

Detail of the stained glass window inside All Hallows, Ringmore. Behind the kneeling figure of a medieval knight can be seen a howitzer and soldiers in Great War uniforms advancing towards the South Devon cliffs and the sea (author's collection)

Annotated Bibliography

Primary sources

Much information was gathered from the local newspapers, particularly the *Kingsbridge and South Devon Gazette*, stored at the Cookworthy Museum in Kingsbridge. Copies of the Ivybridge Parish Magazines were made available by Tom Maddock. Access to the rich archives of Stowford Mill, Ivybridge were made possible by the kind helpfulness of the volunteers of the Ivybridge Heritage Group. The curator of the King's Own Royal Regiment Museum, Lancaster, was of great assistance in helping trace the movements of the 10th King's Own in 1914/15 and providing information about the army career of Horace Backhouse.

Working with old photographs is never easy. The picture on page 78 showing men of the 10th King's Own leaving Kingsbridge is a case in point. David Parker (2013, p53) has this picture as Territorials departing Kingsbridge in 1914. However, there are clues from the picture which seem to question this. First, the soldiers' cap badges do not seem to resemble the circular stars of the Devonshire Regiment. Second, if the picture shows Territorials of the Devonshire Regiment then the occasion would have been August 1914, yet the soldiers are wearing greatcoats and the trees in the background appear to lack leaves. This suggests the photograph was taken in the winter rather than in August. Moreover, the Cookworthy Museum holds an original postcard of this exact scene which provides two further clues. First, the postcard is dated 5 October 1915 so the photograph can be no later than September 1915. Second, the donor of the postcard insists these soldiers are men of the King's Own Regiment.

Considering all of the above, the most likely explanation is that this is a photograph of soldiers of the 10th King's Own Royal Lancaster Regiment leaving Kingsbridge station in February 1915, when many departed to join their 3rd Battalion (not May, when the whole regiment left, as their departure was at night and in any case, the trees would have been in leaf).

Secondary sources

The one recent book consulted was David Parker's *The People of Devon in the First World War*, published in 2013 by the History Press, Stroud. Parker covers the whole county of Devon and so his is a less detailed, but much more wide-ranging work than this. Whilst there is some overlap between his work and this, Parker's focus is on the social impact of the war and has less to say about the military and naval exploits of Devon men. Richard Holmes's *Tommy, The British Soldier on the Western Front 1914-1918* (2004, Harper Collins) was useful in terms of the broader picture of the British Army in the war.

The history of the Devonshire Regiment is relatively rich. W.J.P. Aggett covers the period 1914 to 1919 between two volumes of his compendious *The Bloody Eleventh, History of the Devonshire Regiment* (vol ii 1815-1915 and vol iii 1915-1969). Aggett makes use of C.T. Atkinson, *The Devonshire Regiment 1914-1918* (1923), a book which is worth reading in its own right as Atkinson draws upon the Devonshire Regiment diaries throughout.

Following a lead from the BBC, much was discovered about Dr Arthur Hurst from a recent academic paper published in the *Journal of the History of Medicine and Allied Sciences* (Jones, E [2011] War Neuroses and Arthur Hurst: A Pioneering Medical Film about the Treatment of Psychiatric Battle Casualties).

Local newspapers did not appear to carry stories about the Ivybridge airship, but P. Abbott in *The British Airship at War 1914-18* (1989) includes the story of the SS.42. The internet is rich in details of just about all British naval vessels. More about the explosion in Halifax in which HMS *Highflyer* was sunk will be found in M. Monnon's *Miracles and Mysteries: The Halifax Explosion* (1977).

Index